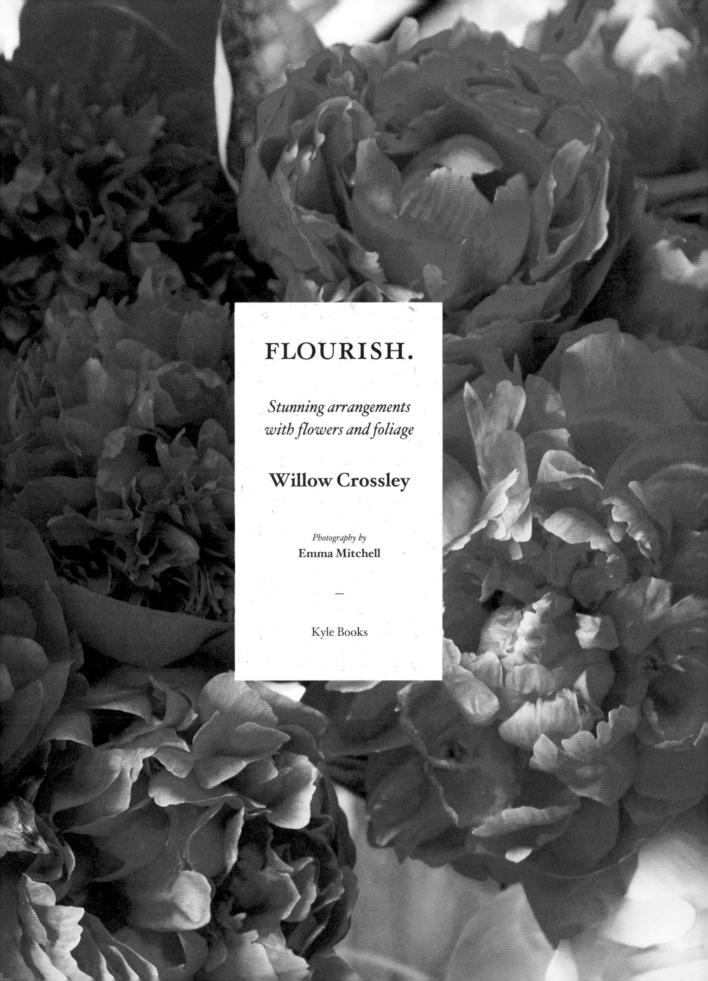

FLOURISH.

*Stunning arrangements
with flowers and foliage*

Willow Crossley

Photography by
Emma Mitchell

—

Kyle Books

For Wolf, Rafferty and Kit,
with all my love   *xxx*

First published in Great Britain in 2016 by
Kyle Books
an imprint of Kyle Cathie Limited
192–198 Vauxhall Bridge Road
London SW1V 1DX
general.enquiries@kylebooks.com
www.kylebooks.co.uk

10 9 8 7 6 5 4 3 2 1

ISBN: 978 0 85783 318 1

A CIP catalogue record for this title is available from the British Library

Willow Crossley is hereby identified as the author of this work
in accordance with Section 77 of the Copyright, Designs and
Patents Act 1988.

Text © Willow Crossley 2016
Photographs © Emma Mitchell 2016
Design © Kyle Books 2016

Editor: Vicky Orchard
Design: Evi O.
Photography: Emma Mitchell
Styling: Willow Crossley
Production: Lisa Pinnell

Colour reproduction by ALTA London
Printed and bound in China by 1010 International Printing Ltd.

INTRODUCTION

I've written about craft and about interiors, about nature and decorating, but it's the floral side of things that really excites me. Since leaving the University of the Arts in London, my careers have been varied. First, there was fashion and beauty, followed by personal shopping and styling, then, more recently, writing and crafting. Writing my second book, *Inspire*, I spent a heavenly year playing around with nature, but it was when I began to work on the 'Flora' chapter that I felt I'd hit gold. It sounds cheesy but coming home from the flower markets or hedgerows with armfuls of flowers, I felt transported by an extraordinary, contented calmness. A rare feeling, living in a house full of small boys.

After realising this new-found love, I enrolled myself on an intensive course at the Covent Garden Academy of Flowers in London. I left convinced that I had found my calling. A month later I found myself standing in a church, face to face with a ginormous pedestal, doing one of my best friend's wedding flowers. Admittedly this time I had my mother as my calming sidekick. She had in fact done all the hard parts – the calculating and ordering – but it was the start. Being in charge of the way someone's wedding looks is a huge responsibility and one that I took incredibly seriously. There were many midnight panics and many doubting moments but when it came down to it, I adored every second. Working with flowers is very physical and sometimes a pretty exhausting job, especially when pregnant as I was when I started out, but I have never done a more rewarding, satisfying, pride-inducing job in my life. And I haven't looked back since.

So, I now call myself a florist. Or a 'floral stylist' if I'm being pernickety. My dream is one day to have a shop, but for now I work from my studio at home, outside but under cover in our converted store. I love how no job is ever the same – the chance for boredom is non-existent. I might be working on a wedding or a dinner, a shop launch or a tea party or filling people's houses with flowers for the weekend. Each task is a fresh challenge and means I need my creative hat on at all times.

(*continued*)

My style of arranging is very wild and natural. I'm not good at tight, neat, symmetry. Foliage is key; the more the better. I often have big containers at home filled with just foliage, no flowers. In early spring, bringing in embryonic branches is magical. And an excellent biology lesson for small people too. Fast forward six months and the fresh limey greens have been replaced with deep reds and oranges. Just as heavenly.

I grew up in the Welsh countryside which at the time, I wasn't crazy about. More and more though, I'm beginning to realise how, even if it was sub-consciously, growing up there has influenced so much of my working style. Whenever I return, I feel so inspired by the rugged wildness and huge sweeping landscapes, by the frothy silvery lichen that carpets the woodland floors, the magical clumps of ferns and the larch branches scattering the pathways. Wherever you look, there's *something* to inspire. Whether it's an actual *thing* or just the shapes and forms created by nature itself. Every time I come home from Wales my arrangements seem to be just that little bit bigger and wilder than before.

In this book, I want to show you how bringing flowers into your home can be so life-enhancing. I'm not saying that they have to be masterly, beautifully designed creations. Just a couple of branches or a few wispy stems in a vase makes all the difference. I want to inspire you to think differently when it comes to choosing flowers and colours. There is far more out there than the supermarkets offer. If you have a friendly local florist, get to know them. Ask them to order things in for you if they don't have it already. Go for walks in your local parks and woodlands, look at the way the plants and trees grow in their natural habitat, study their shapes, their colours and tone. I feel strongly that arrangements should look as natural as possible.

Containers are a huge part of flower arranging. Jam jars for example, one of my constant accessible fallbacks, can look great dotted down the table for a relaxed lunch but would be underwhelming for wedding flowers in a huge church – they'd be swallowed up in all that space.

I want to encourage you to think about the container as much as the flowers and to use something you wouldn't usually think of as a vase or container. Make it a game – everywhere you go, try to find the oddest thing you can (see page 186).

I hope that you will find this book practical, inspiring and easy to use. I want to shake off the notion that flowers are 'hard' to do. They're really not, they just take practice and a bit of patience. There is an infinite supply of life-enhancing ingredients that will unfailingly light up your rooms with scent and colour to brighten your days.

MY HERO FLOWERS

For each season, there are a group of flowers that I always seem to fall back on.
They are my go-tos, the ones that I know 100 per cent will make the arrangement
work. I don't have to have *just* the hero flowers, one or two is enough,
but as long as I've got some of them, I know it'll be a good day!

- SPRING -

Spiraea *Spiraea* 'Grefsheim'

Foxgloves *Digitalis*

Solomon's seal *Polygonatum multiflorum*

Anemones *Anemone coronaria/
A. blanda/A. nemorosa*

Ranunculus

Tulips

Icelandic poppies *Papaver nudicaule*

Lilac *Syringa vulgaris*

- SUMMER -

White gaura *Gaura lindheimerei*

Delphiniums and Larkspur
Consolida ajacis

Peonies

Guelder rose *Viburnum opulus* 'Roseum'

Lady's mantle *Alchemilla mollis*

Cow parsley *Anthriscus sylvestris*

Garden Roses

- AUTUMN -

Dahlias

Hydrangeas
Hydrangea macrophylla/ H. paniculata

Japanese anemones
Anemone hupehensis var. japonica

- WINTER -

Narcissi

Anemones *Anemone coronaria*

Ranunculus

Eucalyptus

dried Hydrangea

Lilac *Syringa vulgaris*
(I use imported lilac in winter)

- FAVOURITE FOLIAGE/FILLERS -

Solomon's seal *Polygonatum multiflorum*

Lamb's ear *Stachys byzantina*

Bupleurum
Bupleurum rotundifolium 'Griffithii'

Eucalyptus

Box (*Buxus*)

variegated Ivy *Hedera helix* 'Caecilia'

Smoke bush *Cotinus obovatus*

Sage *Salvia officinalis*

Heuchera

Geranium leaves

green and copper Beech
Fagus sylvatica/F. purpurea

Oak (*Quercus*)

Stephanandra
Stephanandra incisa

(1)

Spring

ALSO KNOWN AS

Anemone coronaria
'De Caen'
Anemone nemorosa
(Windflower)
Vase life 10 days

1

Anemones

Poppy flowering anemones ('De Caen' varieties) are an early spring highlight.
They are so cheery when you really want some intense colour in your life.
Part of the same family as buttercups, the wild ones are known as windflowers.

Anemones come in saturated, glossy jewel colours – amethyst purples,
garnet and ruby reds and pinks, but my favourites are the white ones with
a velvety black middle. Sometimes you find one or two in a 'white' batch that
look as if their petal tips have been painted with splashes of bright red and these
ones make me incredibly happy. Unlike some of the garden-grown varieties,
which can have hopelessly short stems, 'De Caen' anemones have long stems
which makes them very handy for arranging. Once in the water they continue
to flex their petals and their stems lean in all directions so an arrangement tends
to change its shape overnight. Either enjoy the natural wildness or take this into
account when you're deciding what to put them in and where to place them.
Or, just keep your snips handy and cut them down slightly if they get too unruly
for your liking.

Coloured glasses or Moroccan tea lights make great containers for
anemones. Try them dotted down a kitchen table, a mishmash of colours and
heights. Anemones are thirsty creatures, so keep water levels topped up and
they can last a good ten days.

There are many more varieties of anemones than the bright, single colour
ones but they're not readily available. If you can, do try to grow your own. That
way you can get your hands on the exciting stripy ones, such as *Anemone coronaria
bicolor* 'De Caen' and *A. coronaria* 'Hollandia'.

These jewel-coloured vintage brush pots, handmade by the wonderful Bridie Hall, make the best personalised presents when filled with flowers.

(p. 15)
SPRING

2

Ranunculus

You could be forgiven for mistaking a ranunculus for a rose. These delicate pompom-shaped heads, crammed with pleats of tissue paper-like petals make the most beautiful addition to any arrangement. Showy, long-lasting, not too expensive and appearing in a mouth-watering choice of colours, they are a dream.

Ranunculus start life as tight little balls and then open up, layer by layer, getting frillier and frillier as the days go by. Their petal count is phenomenal. I love the fancy 'Picotee' forms, some with variegated petals and others looking as if they've been dipped in ink. 'Purple Picotee' are ridiculously stunning.

Ranunculus have hollow, curvy stems, which means that they will move in an arrangement. They are incredibly thirsty but do not like having too much water. Give them a couple of inches, nothing more and then keep topping them up every day. Their stems will melt and rot if you soak them in too much water.

The arrangement here would work just as well as a hand-tied bouquet (see page 177). If you are going to use ranunculus in a hand-held bouquet, make sure that it's the foliage or some of the other stronger-stemmed flowers that are in contact with the string you tie it all together with. Ranunculus stems are so fragile and will snap easily.

ALSO KNOWN AS

Ranunculus asiaticus
Persian buttercup
Vase life up to 2 weeks

RANUNCULUS

(*continued*)

[p. **19**]
SPRING

ingredients.

Snips/secateurs

Gold mirrored glass fishbowl
vase (you can, of course,
use a different vase. I just
loved using the mirror so
you could see the underside
of the flowers too.)

30 stems Ranunculus,
both 'Picotee' and plain
varieties – I have used
burgundy, pinks and whites

10 stems Scabious *Scabiosa
atropurpurea* 'Ace of Spades'

20 white Anemones
with a black eye

10 stems Bupleurum

1. Remove all the leaves from the ranunculus stems and lay out
   your conditioned flowers (see page 174) into families on a table
   in front of you.

2. Start by arranging the flowers into a hand-tied posy using the
   spiralling technique (see page 178). Don't use all the flowers
   in the posy, keep back 10–15 stems. When you are happy with
   how they look in your hand, cut them to the desired length
   – it's better to keep them too long than too short – and drop
   into the vase.

3. I always find that round, bowl vases need a lot more flowers
   than you'd expect. When you drop your posy into the vase,
   they all splay out to the sides and you're left with a huge gaping
   hole in the middle. This is why you keep some flowers back
   so that you can fill in the hole with your leftover flowers and
   move them around until you are happy with how they look.
   Remember not to add too much water to the vase and check
   on water levels every day.

3

Blossom

Nothing heralds the arrival of spring quite like a mass of blossom. That first sighting triggers an endorphin rush and I mentally start peeling off my winter layers and unpacking summer sandals on the spot. Blowsy, beautiful and attention-grabbing, blossom is a sensation for eye-catching, dramatic displays.

The season generously lasts for months on end, starting slowly in late winter with a few winter flowering cherries, then blackthorn blooms brighten up the hedgerows and early spring is lit up with the wonderful whites of pear, damson and plums before moving into the heavenly pinks of many different flowering cherries.

The one downside to many blossoms is that, once picked, they don't last particularly long. In water, you'll get up to five days' vase life but out of water, as in this display, you'll only get a day or so. If you pick them while they are still in bud they give you a couple more days as they open on the branch.

For slightly longer-lasting flowers, the ornamental quince *Chaenomeles* is an early spring joy with apple blossom-shaped petals and a huge range of colours ranging from the palest of whites, through to coral and deep rust red. We have some growing up a wall at home that I allow myself to pick on special occasions. (It's a very small plant!)

The blossom used here is an early spring cherry blossom from a tree in our garden, *Prunus x subhirtella* 'Autumnalis Rosea'. Being out of water meant that its lifespan was short, no more than a day, but while it lasted it was a sensation. The gnarly, irregularity of the branches gave shape and movement as well as providing handy little angles to loop other blooms onto.

The key to a hanging is to make the base super sturdy. The base of this one is made from branches of larch, lots of which are covered in wonderful lichen and mini fir cones. The joy of these hangings is that you can make them any size you like – they also look great suspended over tables and could happily grace a wedding or special occasion dinner.

ALSO KNOWN AS

Prunus / Malus / Pyrus

BLOSSOM

(continued)

**4 branches of blossom –
the size you want your hanging
will dictate their size**

4 larch branches

**2 lengths of ribbon -
I used 2m of burgundy
velvet ribbon**

Secateurs

Green waxed wire

1. Lay your sticks and twigs out on the floor in the shape you want to create.

2. Next, wire or tie them all together. I used green, waxed wire as it's easy to camouflage.

3. When you have the base all strung together, take your ribbon and work out the length you want it to be before tying it to each end. I've used a dark burgundy velvet.

4. Personally, I find it easiest to work with hangings from this point onwards when they are in situ. You can always make the base way before you want to display it as well.

5. Now is the time to add the fresh bits. I've used blossoms and eucalyptus. You can use stub wire to attach them or simply slot them in as I've done.

6. If you want to keep the hanging on display for a few days or longer, just remove the bits that aren't looking their best, as and when and add fresh bits in their place.

7. Also, keep in mind water vials for keeping flowers fresh for free-standing structures like this; they will become your best friends at times like these. To use a water vial, simply remove the rubber lid/seal, fill it with water, put the cap back on and then slip the stem into the hole provided in the top of the lid. Top up if the water level decreases.

4

Fritillaries

Daintily suspended below their arching stems, fritillaries are like living artworks. With their unique chequered pattern and nodding cup-shaped heads it's plain where the 'snake's head' name came from. Before the Second World War, England in the spring was full of fritillary meadows. Sadly they're not that common any more, but there is, however, one at Magdalen College, Oxford which just happens to be on my doorstep.

I don't know if it's their regal purple-ness or their wispy frailness but something makes me feel fritillaries deserve their own space; somewhere they can be properly admired and appreciated. A few stems held in antique cut glass can't really be beaten. You only need a few stems. Less can definitely be more here, although they can also look equally ravishing with company.

Here I've recreated what I did at a spring lunch for British brand Mulberry: hundreds of jam jars dotted down the middle of the showroom table filled with white lilac, white ranunculus, *Ammi majus*, white anemones with black middles, lime-green Guelder rose and these wondrous snake's heads for a splash of colour. A spring dream. These arrangements are practically replicas, the only difference is that I swapped the Guelder rose for home-grown hellebores.

After I made this arrangement, I went away for two days and the flowers completely ran out of water. They looked dead as a dodo and I was about to throw them out when I noticed one of the anemones was still looking quite perky. So I thought on the off chance, I'd just give them one more drink. Five hours later both the anemones and fritillaries were as good as new. So don't be fooled by their apparent frailness – they're tougher than they look.

ALSO KNOWN AS

Fritillaria meleagris
**Chequered Lily, Chess flower,
Snake's head fritillary
Vase life 6–8 days**

(p. **26**)
SPRING

Spring in a vase:
hellebores, snake's head
fritillaries, anemones and
white syringa.

5

Waxflower

There's never any worry that waxflowers won't perform on the night. These low-key, native Australian wild flowers are a dream for arranging. They can last up to three weeks and wilting is not a word in their dictionary. With their needle-like leaves and tiny hooked flowers they come in a range of pretty pinky, purple and white tones. They are especially handy in mid-winter when you want a little bit of colour and for things to last that little bit longer than usual. They're also an excellent filler.

I've made them into candle bobeches here – basically, candlestick decorations. If you mist them with water and keep them cool they should last at least a couple of days so you can make them in advance of any occasion that you'd like to use them for.

[p. 28]
SPRING

ALSO KNOWN AS

Chamelaucium uncinatum
Geraldton waxflower
Vase life 2–3 weeks

WAXFLOWER

(continued)

(p. **31**)
SPRING

ingredients.

Covered wire

Snips/ secateurs

Waxflowers
Chamelaucium uncinatum

Stub wire

**Candlesticks with a ledge
for the bobeche to rest on**

Candles

1. Make a circle the required size by wrapping the covered
    wire around itself in a ring until it feels sturdy.

2. Snip off lengths of the waxflower about 8cm long. Wire a few
    of the small lengths together and then, with another piece of
    stub wire, wire this onto the circlet you've made.

3. Continue, making mini little groupings and attaching them to
    the ring until it's totally covered. You don't want to have any
    wire on show. I like mine to look quite wild and wayward.

4. If you are making them in advance, keep them alive by misting
    with water regularly or even better, keep them under damp
    layers of tissue paper until you are ready to use them.

6

Tulips

This might be a bit of a sweeping generalisation but I find men aren't big tulip fans. So often, when I'm making a male-ordered bouquet, their only stipulation is 'no tulips'. I have to resist with all my might not to shout and scream from the rooftops about how wonderful they are and remind myself the customer is always right.

I put it down to the association with unfortunate weedy tulip combinations on garage forecourts or those repetitive front gardens full of poker straight red and yellow blobs you see in spring. So, to be fair, if this is all you know perhaps their lack of love is not so surprising.

Once upon a time in seventeenth-century Holland, tulip bulbs were such highly prized possessions that each one would be traded for *thousands* of pounds in a frenzy that was known as tulip mania. Luckily for us, times have changed and they're rather more affordable today. Tulips are an enormous family, related to the lily, and there are an almost bewildering number of varieties – so I would eat my hat if I couldn't find *one* to please the doubting Thomases.

Seek out the crazy, frilly, striped parrot varieties. The crazier the better. The white and raspberry streaked 'Rem's Favourite' brings so much joy to a kitchen table. For a slightly more subtle moment, there's a pale green and pink striped sensation called 'Green Wave' or consider the lily-flowered 'China Pink', or tall 'White Triumphator' with their elegantly reflexed petals that open out into flat star shapes. One of the joys of tulips is their long life in a vase – up to two weeks – alongside their habit of starting cup-shaped, then gradually unfurling and finally dropping their petals one by one. They have a very graceful way of dying. ➤

ALSO KNOWN AS

Tulipa

Vase life 1 week

TULIPS

(continued)

There are too many beauties to name them all individually. The key when arranging with tulips is to mix colours and varieties. Clashing combinations are irresistible, especially with lime-green euphorbia or alchemilla that make their rich colours really glow. Try a maroon-purple 'Havran' with a flame orange 'Prinses Irene' and brightest pink 'Chato' or 'Candy Cane'. For a red clash try the delicious scented (rare in a tulip) orange 'Ballerina' lily flower with the fattest double-flowered 'Uncle Tom' and 'Abigail' or 'Antraciet'. Less shouty, but intriguing is the huge peony tulip 'La Belle Epoque', a faded peachy coral that seems to have come straight from a Dutch painting.

I prefer a huge bunch of tulips rather than a few singular stems dotted around. Large vintage jugs and old ceramic cachepots work particularly well to display them in. A line of vintage enamel spice tins also looks fabulous if you have a *lot* of tulips.

7

Alliums

Essentially giant pompoms, alliums come in every tone of purple you can imagine as well as white and yellow and can be any size from a gobstopper to a basketball. They are a joy to work with. They last well – up to two weeks – and work brilliantly as both filler and as standalone showstoppers. Even after they've died they look just as wonderful as spiky, sculptural arrangements. Being part of the onion family – they're known as 'ornamental onions' – they do have a downside. They smell. But this is easily remedied with frequent water changing, or a splash of bleach in the water if the size of the arrangement makes changing the water tricky.

With this in mind, try to use alliums more in outdoor arrangements. This arrangement would be perfect for a summer lunch party. There are five different varieties of allium: 'Globemaster', 'Drumstick', *Allium. aflatunense*, 'Giganteum' and 'Purple Sensation' (also known as *A. hollandicum*). I've displayed them in an old, vibrant-blue milk churn. Milk churns make fabulous containers for large-scale arrangements, the only thing you need to keep in mind is that if they are old they are likely to be full of holes and covered in rust. Flowers do not like rust. But they do like water, so you'll need to use a liner inside the churn. You can get proper green plastic vase liners online or at garden centres or improvise using yogurt pots or ice-cream tubs or small buckets – anything you can get your hands on that fits into the churn; they're not going to be seen, after all.

ALSO KNOWN AS

Ornamental onions

Vase life up to 2 weeks

ALLIUMS

(continued)

1 vintage milk churn

1 plastic liner to fit inside
the milk churn. If you can't
source one that fits perfectly,
fill the bottom of the churn
with something until you get
enough height to rest the liner
on it. Logs or folded cardboard
or tins would all work fine.

Snips/secateurs

15 'Globemaster' alliums

15 'Drumstick' alliums

18 'Purple Sensation' alliums

15 *Allium aflatunense*

10 *Allium giganteum*

1. Please don't follow the quantities above too religiously but use
    them as a guide. I have used a large churn but you can use any
    container you like, its size will dictate how many alliums you
    will want. Beautiful, tall olive oil drums would also look fab.
    I wanted quite a dense, full arrangement so crammed as many
    alliums in as I could fit, but it would also look great with more
    space between the heads.

2. Consider where the arrangement is going be placed. Is it going
    to be seen from 360 degrees or just front on? If it's going to be
    as large as this one, put it where it's going to be displayed and
    work on it from there.

3. Start by placing the biggest alliums into the container
    first. Continue adding the flowers, decreasing in head size,
    filling in the spaces. Keep standing back and looking at the
    arrangement as a whole, from all angles. I wanted an explosion
    effect, so made some stems long and others much shorter.

4. Carry on adding stems; you may want to take some out and
    trim them or move them around – don't be afraid to take your
    time and play around. Allium stems are pretty robust so can
    take a bit of adjustment if needs be.

ALSO KNOWN AS

Digitalis purpurea
Vase life up to 2 weeks

8

Foxgloves

Foxgloves make the most brilliant, showstopping centrepieces for weddings and parties. The deep pink ones that grow in the wild are lovely but sometimes their strong colour can be tricky to mingle with other flowers. I'd suggest arranging them by themselves or just with leafy oak branches in a huge bucket. When there's a choice of foxgloves, try a white with dotted purple insides or the soft pink 'Sutton's Apricot'. These work as beautifully in a smaller bouquet arrangement as they do in a full-blown showstopper.

The foxgloves in this arrangement are actual plants. Not only will they last longer than cut flowers but they can also be planted in the garden once they've peaked and should (hopefully) reappear the following spring.

This project is not remotely tricky but I wanted to show how easy it is to create something so striking with so little effort. I have used eight robust plants. Choose yours carefully, look for as many stems and as much foliage as possible, the fuller and more lush looking the better. Leave them in their pots so that they can be lifted in and out for a drink every couple of days into a sinkful of water. Watering this way creates far less mess than with a can.

Sat in vintage wooden apple crates on somewhere like a hall table – cool and shady – they are just as they like to be. As much as they look stunning displayed in lovely old china jugs, housing them in wood gives them the look of coming straight from the wild. They make great party decorations – placed on the floor, beside a drinks table or lining a church path for a summer wedding.

To use them as cut stems for a beautiful bouquet, mix some native *Digitalis purpurea* with some 'Sutton's Apricot' foxgloves, add frothy white *Ammi majus*, cream *Astrantia major*, pale lilac delphiniums, Solomon's seal and 'Coral Charm' coral pink peonies.

If you are cutting from your garden, sit foxgloves in a bucket of warm water for a couple of hours by themselves before arranging. The plants are slightly toxic so make sure you wash your hands after handling them and keep them away from small people.

(p. **43**)
SPRING

9
Icelandic Poppies

These beauties get a place in my top three flowers and are a 'go-to' when you really want to wow. It feels like Christmas when they arrive, all wrapped up in their special protective papers, their papery petals still cocooned inside green furry hoods.

It's tempting to display them alone so you can really appreciate their beauty. But after many an experiment, I think that they work best with some friends by their sides, even if it's just a few as in this arrangement.

Unlike lots of poppy varieties including opium poppies, *Papaver somniferum,* which are grown for their seeds and pods and whose billowing petals last barely a day once cut, imported Icelandic poppies make *great* cut flowers. Their elegant long, leafless stems are tough and sturdy and can last up to a week with good care. When they come from Holland they tend to arrive as closed buds but will unfurl incredibly quickly in front of your eyes if you bring them into a warm home. Early in the morning they can be totally clamped shut but two hours later after hanging out next to the Aga half of them will be fully open, crinkly petals raring to go. ➤

(p. **45**)
SPRING

ALSO KNOWN AS

Papaver nudicaule
Vase life 5–7 days

ICELANDIC
POPPIES

(continued)

Icelandic poppies tend to come in a bunch of mixed colours including satsuma orange, pale peach, white and canary yellow. This arrangement is meant to feel clean and fresh so rather than adding lots more colour, keep it simple with white ranunculus and the Amazon lily *Eucharis grandiflora*. The latter is part of the amaryllis family and you can also use this when you want something a little special, its thick waxy petals and thick hollow stems feel rather sumptuous. Until recently I actually presumed it belonged to the orchid family as its exotic looks imply they could definitely be related.

Both the poppies and the lilies have lovely long stems and it seems a pity to cut them down. For a tall elegant display I've chosen two narrow ribbed glass candleholders that handily double up nicely as vases. The arrangements feel very wayward and out of control, almost like living artworks as each time a poppy bursts open the composition moves and pleasingly changes shape.

10

Solomon's Seal

Finding the first Solomon's seal of the season is cause for major excitement. Growing in shady parts of the garden in the early spring, they are extremely versatile and I try to use them in every arrangement I possibly can while they are in season. There's something so peaceful about them, the graceful curve of the arched stem and the tiny, elegant, green tipped, white bellflowers. They look just as ravishing standing tall en masse in exploding, fountain-style arrangements as they do cut down and mixed in with some other spring companions.

Here they're mixed with Guelder rose and white foxgloves. The spires of the foxgloves contrast with the round spheres of Guelder rose and the Solomon's seal acts as the soothing balance in the middle.

(p. 49)
SPRING

Try a combination of Solomon's seal, 'Coral Sunset' peonies, lilac and blue delphiniums and pale pink larkspur. The colours work together so well and the clean, bright, green and little white bells of the Solomon's seal add a vibrant freshness that is hard to rival.

ALSO KNOWN AS

Polygonatum multiflorum

Vase life 7 days

SOLOMON'S SEAL

(continued)

ingredients.

Snips/secateurs

A large, narrow-necked glass vase

5 foxgloves *Digitalis purpurea*

3 stems Guelder rose *Viburnum opulus* 'Roseum'

11 stems Solomon's seal *Polygonatum multiflorum*

1. Condition your flowers (see page 174) and then sort them into families on a table in front of you.

2. This arrangement began life as a hand-tied posy so start with a foxglove as the leading flower and take it in your left hand (if you are left-handed, do the reverse). Next, take a Guelder rose stem and sit it on top of the foxglove so they are diagonally overlapping. With your spare hand, turn the bouquet, then add a stem of Solomon's seal. This turning action makes the stems form a spiral shape, which in turn makes it easier and neater to add, adjust or remove stems. Keep adding the stems, remembering to turn after each new addition.

3. When you have used up all your flowers or you're happy with the size of the bouquet, hold it out in front of you to get a good look at the whole form. Now's the time to adjust any lengths. When you are happy with the heights, cut the stems to the length you require. My general rule of proportion is that the arrangement should be 2½ times the height of the vase. To be on the safe side, err on the side of caution and first cut longer than you think you need – you can always make the stems shorter.

4. Drop the flowers into the vase and let them fall into place naturally. You can now play with them, adding or taking away anything you like until the arrangement is just as you want.

Sometimes some of the lower bells will turn brown and crinkly before others – don't throw them away, simply snip them off and carry on enjoying them.

11

Guelder Roses

One of the joys of these lime-green pompoms is their shape. In any arrangement, rather like in a garden border, you need a mix of shape and texture, which this flower has in abundance. Their forms bring lacy softness and curves to any party. The vibrancy of the lime seems to brighten an arrangement, no matter the occasion. The colour seems to lift its companions at any season and Guelder rose works well alongside lilac, tulips, cabbage roses, anemones and spires of delphiniums.

Despite the common name, Guelder roses are viburnums, not roses. Like syringa, viburnum have hard woody stems that do need some attention before being played around with. Their frilly leaves are so pretty that it feels a shame to strip them off, but after much experimenting, I've learnt that the blooms do behave a lot better without them. If you keep them on, it seems that the water goes to the leaves rather than the flower heads and the flowers die horribly quickly. Leaf removal ensures that the flowers get a drink and will stay perky. Make you sure you cut the stems at an angle and make a 5cm slit up the stem so that they can drink more easily. Sear the stems by dunking them into a few centimetres of boiling water for 45 seconds, then give them a long cool drink in a bucket or sink of water, up to their necks for at least a couple of hours, overnight if possible. They should be able to last up to two weeks if you condition them properly like this.

ALSO KNOWN AS

Viburnum opulus 'Roseum'
Green pompom bush,
Snowball bush
Vase life 2 weeks

12

Lilac

Lilac is one of my hero flowers. The season is short but glorious. For a spring wedding, I use it to make bouquets which are full of this visionary beauty. Packed with clouds of 'Maiden's Blush' lilac, deliciously scented David Austin 'Patience' roses, Icelandic poppies for a splash of colour, Guelder rose, alchemilla and spirea for a bit of wayward wisp, it was a bit of a struggle saying goodbye to this arrangement.

There's something so sumptuous and luxurious about lilac. It instantly makes an arrangement feel more special. With hundreds of tiny umbels forming every fluffy panicle, each bloom looks like a starry constellation. The difference between common lilac that grows in gardens in late spring and the commercially grown variety is mostly the scent. Home-grown blooms smell quite sublime. Heavenly. Another difference is that commercially grown stems are poker straight and tall unlike their garden cousins whose stems are more twiggy and angular, making arranging more of a challenge.

Lilac makes the most fantastic cut flower but you do need to do a few key things to ensure it lasts well. Remove all leaves from the stem, and if you are picking it from your garden, sear 10 per cent of the stem in boiling water for 30 seconds then plunge stems into cold, deep water, and leave in the dark for as long as you can, ideally overnight.

This arrangement should feel very elegant and calm. The colours are tonal and simple, lots of green and white from lilac and Guelder rose and blossom, but with a gentle splash of colour from the Icelandic poppies.

ALSO KNOWN AS

Syringa vulgaris
Vase life 4–5 days

Old folklore believes that bringing lilac into the house is unlucky; some associate it with death as it was used to line coffins to mask the smell. Others believe that Victorian gardeners just made up the rumour to stop people picking it from their trees!

(2)

Summer

13

Hollyhocks

Despite being natives of Asia, to me, hollyhocks are a quintessentially English flower. Think of those Victorian watercolours of cottage gardens where hollyhocks cluster picturesquely below thatched roofs. I live in the Cotswolds where during the summer months it can feel quite like a hollyhock theme park. Almost every single honey-coloured cottage is fenced in by crowds of the towering spires. I've always rather ignored them until last summer when I met a beautiful, almost black version – *Alcea rosea* 'Nigra'. I'm now hooked and delight in dreaming up enormous arrangements with them as the leading ladies. Saying that, as much as it feels wasteful to cut them down in size, they do work really well as shorter stems.

In this arrangement, none of them were especially tall, which made them quite manageable. Often, they grow so vigorously in hot dry summers – over 3 metres – that parts of them can understandably get rather worse for wear. There is also the threat of hollyhock rust that attacks the leaves, not the flowers, luckily, but it makes stems look pretty ropey. However, the joy of them being such giants is that there will usually be some parts that are salvageable.

This display is very pink and very girly. It's also very wild and looks quite like the garden has sprung in from the outside window. It would work really well as a long centrepiece like this for a wedding or a party.

ALSO KNOWN AS

Alcea rosea
Vase life 5–7 days

In the language of flowers, hollyhocks symbolise fruitfulness. They are also the thirteenth wedding anniversary flower.

HOLLYHOCKS

(continued)

ingredients.

4 blocks of floral foam
and tray to hold 4 blocks

Snips/secateurs

9 pink Hydrangeas

10 mixed pink Hollyhocks

10 pink Japanese anemones,
Anemone hupehensis
var. japonica

10 white Japanese anemones,
Anemone x hybrida
'Honorine Jobert'

9 pink Scabious
Scabiosa columbaria 'Pink Mist'

5 pink Echinacea
Echinacea purpurea 'Maxima'

1. Start by soaking the floral foam blocks in a bucket or sink full of water – avoid pushing them down but let them absorb the water in their own time. The blocks should be filled with water after about 10 minutes.

2. Transfer the blocks to the tray and use pot tape to secure them to the tray.

3. Lay your conditioned flowers (see page 174) on a table in front of you and sort out into flower families.

4. Starting with the hydrangeas, cut the stems at an angle and insert them into the floral foam. Stems need to be kept short and snug to the foam. The hydrangeas will form the base and shape of your arrangement.

5. The base of this arrangement is quite dense with flowers, especially compared to the rest of it, which is airy and light.

6. Cutting all your stems at an angle, add the flowers one by one in decreasing size order, starting with the hollyhocks, stepping back occasionally to give yourself perspective.

7. The aim is for it to look wild. Don't try and make it look too neat but it wants to feel as though you've just dug up a bit of the garden and re-positioned it. If you do choose to place your arrangement on a windowsill, make sure it doesn't sit in full sunlight as this will shorten its life considerably.

(p. 67)
SUMMER

This arrangement would
look beautiful running
down the length of
a dinner table too.
Just remember to vary
the heights so your guests
can see one another
across the table.

14

Agapanthus

My childhood summers were spent on the island of Tresco in the Isles of Scilly. The seas are Caribbean clear, the beaches white and the land between is scattered with drifts of dazzling blue and white agapanthus. They are everywhere. Their showy multi-flowered, pompom heads come in a range of blues from pale sea blue to exotic deep purplish blue as well as bright white, standing tall and perky on thick, poker straight stems.

This arrangement is 'Tresco in a vase', using agapanthus and fiery orange crocosmia. Crocosmia are as ubiquitous on Tresco as agapanthus; wherever you turn they are never too far apart, growing, it seems, in happy harmony.

(p. **68**)
SUMMER

I've used an antique vase that was allegedly found at the bottom of the sea, in a shipwreck. It's covered in some kind of coral or barnacle-like substance so I like to believe it's true. And what could be more fitting for the flowers?

As well as being displayed like this as a huge bunch of giant starry heads, agapanthus look wonderful arranged as single stems. Think about dotting a line of them down a dinner table or mantelpiece, varying the heights by cutting the stems at different lengths into bottles of mixed sizes.

As the agapanthus start to fade, prolong their life by removing individual wilting petals as they go brown.

ALSO KNOWN AS

Agapanthus africanus
African Lily, Lily of the Nile,
African Blue Lily
Vase life 10 days

15

Garden Rose

Almost everyone adores a rose. Well, most people do. I spoke to a bride last night who announced she didn't like roses and didn't want them anywhere near her wedding. Obviously, I'm now on a mission to change her mind. How on earth can she resist the sheer beauty of a heavenly scented, blowsy garden rose?

I'm presuming she's never come into contact with them. To be fair to her, we could quite happily live without any of the soulless roses you often find in supermarkets or garage forecourts. With their tight buds, stiff stems, solid petals and waxy leaves, they could be plastic. So let's pretend that's what the bride is talking about and move onto the proper, beautiful garden roses that you can't *not* love.

It's the blowsy, fullness of true garden roses that will seduce you with the gentle, delicate frills of the petals. Topping off such perfection the best of them have an intoxicating scent that you'll want to bottle. And you'll love the transformation from bud to open rose such as the heavenly way the almost green buds of the *Rosa* 'Margaret Merril' unfurl into a white bowl-shaped rose with gold stamens. Most rose buds, including the dark crimson 'William Lobb', are enveloped by a nubby green calyx before they open into flat saucer-shaped purple flowers. Alba roses, such as the pale pink 'Queen of Denmark', have a perfect scent and useful grey green leaves. Centifolia roses, sometimes known unglamorously as cabbage roses, have the fullest flowers that start life cup-shaped and then seem forced open by their volume of petals. 'Fantin-Latour' is one such beauty. ➤

(p. **73**)
SUMMER

ALSO KNOWN AS

Cabbage rose

Provence rose

'English Rose'

Vase life 5 days

GARDEN ROSE

(continued)

David Austin is perhaps the most well-known rose breeder in England. In the 1970s he started a whole new genre of 'English Roses' at his nursery in Shropshire by crossing old varieties with modern hybrid teas and floribunda roses. His mission was to breed modern roses that looked and smelt like old-fashioned cottage varieties but were healthier and repeat flowered through the summer. If I won the lottery my house would be filled with his creations 24/7. Sadly they're not that easy to get hold of unless you grow your own. Florists and supermarkets rarely have them for sale. It's all down to costs. The more robust, hybrid tea varieties like the 'Avalanche' that you see are all flown in from sunnier climes, most notably Kenya, where they can be grown on a vast scale. Saying that, more cottage-style roses are now coming out of Kenya but they lack the scent of the British-grown ones.

If you can't grow them yourself, do ask your local florist or even better find a local grower.

MY FAVOURITE ROSES

'Joie de Vivre'
Beautifully scented, soft peach and pale pink blooms.

'Burgundy Ice'
Dark plum vision.

'Margaret Merril'
Cream with gold stamens and a gorgeous scent.

'Constance Spry'
Cup-shaped pink with intense myrrh scent.

'Ferdinand Pichard'
Striped crimson and white – show-stopping in a vase.

'Charles Rennie Mackintosh'
Lilac rose that fades in colour elegantly with a delicious almond scent.

HAND-TIED
ROSE BOUQUET

ingredients.

Small sharp knife

9 garden roses

9 stems Chocolate Cosmos
Cosmos atrosanguineus

**7 (minimum) scented
Geranium leaves**
Pelargonium graveolens

7 (minimum) stems Mint

1. I love using scented foliage in an arrangement. Geranium leaves and mint are two of my favourites. I wish this book had a 'scratch and sniff' option – the scent of this bouquet was indescribably delicious.

2. The one disadvantage with garden roses, unlike their ram-rod straight cousins, is that they can have weak stems. The heads are often so petal-heavy that they become rather wobbly. Take this into account when you start arranging. Use the geranium leaves as support for your roses, keeping them on the outside.

3. Condition all the flowers (see page 174), and remove the thorns from the roses by slicing them off carefully with a sharp knife. Then sort them into families on a table in front of you.

4. Take one of the biggest roses in your left hand (opposite if you are left-handed); this will become the centre of the bouquet. Next add one of the chocolate cosmos, placing the stem diagonally on top of the rose. Turn the flowers with your right hand. If you want to create a domed effect, keep adding the flowers slightly lower each time. Always turn in the same direction. This forms a spiral shape and makes it easy to add or remove any wayward stems. Then add some mint or geranium leaves, continuing to add on a diagonal. Turn the bouquet each time you add a stem. The stems will begin to fan out creating a spiral effect. This strengthens the arrangement and also lets you reposition the flowers if you need to, simply by pulling them up or down.

5. Add the blooms until you have used them all up. Keep your hands relaxed as you add the flowers, this will let you adjust more easily.

6. When you are happy with the shape and size of the bouquet, wrap a length of raffia or string around the top of the binding point, just above your hands, and tie in a knot to hold it all together. Trim the ends of the stems straight across so that the bunch can stand upright in a vase and all the stems will be in water. The spiral formation means it will stand beautifully.

7. To keep the arrangement going for as long as possible, keep out of direct sunlight, away from any draughts and add some plant food.

16
Passionflower

I find passionflowers are interesting more for their rambling, vine-like foliage than their starry purple blooms. One wall of our house is covered with passionflower and I love how it constantly changes. There are so many visible stages in its year. One minute it has ornate milky green buds and in seemingly no time these morph into purple explosions of flower that then turn into egg-shaped, bright orange fruits. As well as its use in flower arrangements, the fruit can also be eaten and people have used it medicinally for years to help with stress and anxiety. So it's far more than just a pretty face.

Passionflower is a self-clinging climber that clambers via tendrils. This provided hours of entertainment when I was little – if you carefully unpeeled the tendrils and attached them somewhere else they'd carry on growing. It was like having your very own green pet.

Here they are used to dress an outside dinner table. As they were out of water they didn't last much longer than the dinner itself, but spritzing them every so often prolonged the inevitable wilting.

I wanted to give the impression that the vines were *alive* – part of the table. Rather than just plopping them down the middle of the table, you can weave them in and around the plates and glasses – even attaching tendrils to candlesticks. A few vases of single stems of green hydrangeas added into the mix also give a bit of height. I tried adding the stems of the passionflower to the hydrangea vases as they'd have been happier having a drink but the stems were not supple enough so didn't sit properly.

If you have a staircase with banisters, try weaving lengths of the vine around them for a party. This also works well with trailing ivy – a quick-fix winter garland alternative if you don't have the time, money or energy to do a full-blown fir-filled extravaganza.

ALSO KNOWN AS

Passiflora caerulea
Arrangement life 5 hours

17

Lupins

Not the daintiest flower, lupins are almost sculptural, like elegant Eiffel towers with their pointy spires craning towards the light. They have hollow stems, which does give them a tendency to snap. To prevent this, turn them upside down, fill the stem with tepid water and then plug the base with cotton wool or simply hold your thumb over the end while you put them back into water. Filling them with water expels any air left inside. If you are picking them from your garden, try to put them straight into water when you pick them.

Lupins look their best displayed to stand tall and proud with their many coloured pea-like flowers all jumbled together, the boldest colours sitting next to each other, clashing as much as possible. Their foliage deserves its own attention as the milky green, spiky down-covered leaves are beautiful enough to display alone, they wouldn't look out of place somewhere tropical. They slightly remind me of marijuana leaves but are much, much prettier. (The only downside of home-grown flowers is that their leaves can accumulate a spectacular quantity of greenfly – so if that happens, it's obviously best to strip them off.)

There are two different lupin arrangements here. One is just to illustrate how 'simple' can be so very effective. Take a collection of old glass bottles, a mix of apothecary bottles with small blue and clear glass old medicine bottles. I found most of the medicine bottles while I was walking in the woods – someone had clearly being doing a spot of spring cleaning and thrown a cache of these away. Despite being covered in mud, inside and out, it was like finding the end of a rainbow!

Arranging like this en masse looks good in many different places – dotted down a dining table, along a mantelpiece or a windowsill. Obviously a line of bottles gives the most impact but equally, if space is tight, you can be minimal with one or two vases, which can look just as magical.

The second arrangement requires a bit more effort. It is a perfect early summer creation that mixes gorgeous colour combinations.

ALSO KNOWN AS

....

Lupinus

Bluebonnets, Quaker bonnets

Vase life 4–5 days

LUPINS
(continued)

ingredients.

Snips/secateurs

Chicken wire

Pot tape

Two-handled, cream ceramic
Constance Spry-style vase

7 Lupins in a mix of colours

7 'Coral Sunset' Peonies

5 dark red Peonies 'Red
Charm' or 'Karl Rosenfield'

9 lilac Sweet Peas
Lathyrus odoratus

5 stems Sweet William
Dianthus barbatus,
the brighter the better

5 stems Stephanandra
Stephanandra incisa

(p. **85**)
SUMMER

1. Remove all foliage that will live below the water line and
    then sort the families on a table in front of you.

2. Start by cutting a rectangle of the chicken wire slightly bigger
    than the length of the vase. Make it into a bolster shape and
    push it into the vase. It's absolutely fine for it all to overlap.
    Secure with floral tape by wrapping the tape around both the
    wire and container, finishing on the underside where no one
    can see it.

3. Fill the vase with water, then, remembering to make sure
    the stems are hitting the bottom of the vase so that they can
    drink, start by adding the foliage. This will define the shape
    of your arrangement. I start at the edges and work my way in,
    finishing with the most height in the middle.

4. When you are finished with the foliage, it's time to add your
    main flowers, the lupins and peonies. They will move and
    stretch towards the light over time so be prepared to do a bit
    of fiddling. Now fill in the spaces with your in-betweeners –
    the sweet peas and the Sweet William.

5. Remember to keep checking water levels and topping up
    when needed.

(p. **86**)
SUMMER

Seriously simple, there's
not a lot of arranging to
do here. The choice of
bottles is as important
as the flowers; I've
used my favourite old
apothecary bottles and
a mix of recycled blue glass
medicine bottles. The dark
background adds to the
drama of the lupins.

18

Aquilegia

It's the daintiness of aquilegias that I love so much. Their delicate bonnet-like petals conjure up notions of magic and fairies. Or of Victorian ladies, as 'granny's bonnet' is one of the names they go by, the other two being 'aquilegia' and 'columbine'. *Columbus* in Latin means 'dove' while *aquila* means 'eagle'. Their petals are said to resemble the open wings of the birds and the long, graceful spurs represent their curved heads and necks. They flower in early summer and are a thankful stopgap between the end of the spring flowers and the start of the summery ones.

In this arrangement they are shown off in a mossy table centrepiece with some other spring favourites: foxgloves, *Fritillaria persica*, Solomon's seal and snake's head fritillaries. These mossy wreaths are incredibly easy to create and can be made with almost any flower, providing the stems are strong enough to be poked into oasis.

(p. 88)
SUMMER

ALSO KNOWN AS

Columbine, Granny's bonnet
Vase life 5 days

AQUILEGIA

(continued)

[p. **91**]
SUMMER

ingredients.

Oasis wreath –
this one has a 30cm diameter

3 Foxgloves *Digitalis purpurea*

5 Solomon's seal
Polygonatum multiflorum

5 white Aquilegia

3 purple *Fritillaria persica*

3 Snake's head fritillaries
Fritillaria meleagris

2 *Thalictrum delavayi*
'Splendide white' stems

Sphagnum moss

Mossing pins

1. Make sure you work on a surface that doesn't mind getting wet - i.e. not your best cloth-covered dining table. Working with oasis makes a mess.

2. Condition your flowers (see page 174).

3. Start by dropping the oasis ring into a basin of water and wait until it's fully absorbed the water. Do not push it down to hurry it along.

4. One by one, insert the stems into the oasis, turning the wreath as you go. You want them to appear as if they are growing naturally so, for instance, the foxglove is inserted to look poker straight. The Solomon's seal, on the other hand, grows in a curving habit so is slotted in at an angle.

5. When you have added all your flowers, start introducing the moss, in and around the base of the stems, making sure you cover every bit of oasis. Mossing pins will help to secure any unruly bits – to use them, simply push each one down on top of the bit of moss you want to secure into the oasis. They magically disappear in the moss and hold it all together.

6. Water the wreath every day by misting with water or dropping gently into a sink full of water. Just remember to wait for the wreath to stop dripping before putting it back in situ.

19

Peonies

Everyone loves a peony and I am no exception. Heralding the approaching summer, I adore their silken tissue-papery petals, their voluptuousness and all the sumptuous colours they come in are just beautiful. They start off as retiring tight balls and then unfurl before your eyes into full-blown, ready-to-burst showstoppers. One of my best ever jobs was a summer wedding where the lovely bride wanted to use *only* peonies. The reception was a lunch held in a beautiful orangery with one very long table seating 200 people running through the middle. Needless to say, we needed a *lot* of peonies.

I'd say 80 per cent of my floral life is spent trying to coax flowers to come out on time. Forcing 500 peonies to perform was testing, to put it mildly. Our house was overflowing with buckets of peonies for weeks before the wedding and I spent hours dithering over whether the buckets were happy where they were or would they perhaps be happier somewhere else? There were many nights when I crept downstairs at 3am panicking that the ones in the kitchen were going to overheat. I cannot tell you the relief that on the day, they were all on their best behaviour.

This arrangement works really well in a dining room. I wanted to create an ombré peony river running down the table for a girly dinner party – very simple, pretty and feminine. You do need quite a lot of peonies to create this but a cheaper idea would be to fill in gaps with less expensive tonal blooms, something like a carnation would work well. You can use lots of mini bottles as the containers, mostly milk bottles but also some vintage glass medicine bottles too. It's good to have varying heights.

(p. **94**)
SUMMER

ALSO KNOWN AS

Paeonia lactiflora varieties
Vase life up to 2 weeks

PEONIES

(continued)

〔 p. **97** 〕
SUMMER

ingredients.

Approx. 40–50 small glass bottles, plain, coloured or a mixture – the number you need will depend on how long you want the 'river' to be.

Snips/secateurs

50 PEONIES

IN A RANGE OF COLOURS:

Cream:
'Duchesse de Nemours',
'Bridal Icing', 'Elsa Sass'

Peach:
'Coral Charm', 'Coral Sunset'

Pale pink:
'Albert Crousse',
'Angel Cheeks',
'Sarah Bernhardt',
'Florence Nicholls'

Bright and dark pinks:
'Adolphe Rousseau',
'Barbara', 'Bunker Hill',
'Dr Alexander Fleming',
'Général MacMahon' and
'Inspecteur Lavergne'

Two tone:
'Mr G.F. Hemerik',
'Bowl of Beauty',
'Bowl of Love',
'Celebrity',
'Cora Stubbs' and
'Henri Potin'

20 stems of filler flowers,
such as carnations, roses,
ranunculus, astrantia

1. Start by filling all the bottles with water and dotting them down the table.

2. Cut down your conditioned peonies (see page 174) and drop one into each bottle so the heads are just resting on the neck of each container. The proportions might look a bit odd individually, but if you keep the stems long they don't work so well en masse.

3. Group them in colours, starting with the palest and gradually moving through the colour palette, finishing with the darkest at the far end. When all the bottles are filled, take a step back and look at the table as a whole. The flowers will probably need a bit of moving and shuffling about until they look right.

4. If you leave the display in situ for a while, it will want frequent preening because peonies open up far faster when you cut stems short than if they're left long. This means shapes and colours will change – a peony that was once coral might for example become a clotted cream shade and need moving down to the paler end of the ombré river – it's musical chairs for flowers. This arrangement can last for up to two weeks.

5. A great trick to lure reluctant peonies out is to keep trimming the stems. Every time you snip the stem, a peony will open further.

20
Lysimachia Disco Balls

Lysimachia, or loosestrife, isn't an especially exciting flower. It's definitely not a showstopper but a very useful and pretty filler. And it behaves very well at all times which makes it great for using in this disco ball – no wilting or throwing petals on the floor. These giant pompoms get the most wonderful reaction from people and require relatively little skill to make. The hardest part is stringing up the ball with string and wire at the start.

This ball should feel very natural and wild so keep it quite tonal with lots of greens and whites with a few splashes of burgundy. My lawn is so unkempt, uncut, out-of-control grass covered in little white flowers and clover – this pompom looks slightly as if my garden has just exploded and I've rolled it into a ball and hung it up again.

The base is made with green hydrangea. Not big whole ones, you want to break each head up into little florets and then insert them into the wet floral foam. When the whole ball is covered in hydrangea – no floral foam left on show – you then add the rest of your team. I used white larkspur, *Consolida ajacis*, *Sanguisorba officinalis*, *Gaura lindheimerei*, *Ammi majus* and white veronica.

It's easier to cover the ball with hydrangea before you hang it – do it on a table, resting the ball in a cereal bowl or even perched on top of a tennis ball tube – and then as soon as you've covered the ball, hang it up and then add the remaining ingredients in situ. It does get very heavy so make sure you have tough string and a strong, reliable hook to hang it from. Nothing is worse than finishing your masterpiece then discovering the nail is not strong enough to take the weight as the whole thing smashes to the ground. Or, even worse, all over your beautifully laid dinner table.

The beauty of these disco balls is their chameleon quality – you can make them with almost any flowers in any colour to fit any theme or colour scheme. Roses, carnations, daisies, gypsophila and sunflowers would all make good bases. To prolong their life, invest in a water mister as spraying them every day does help them look their best for longer.

ALSO KNOWN AS

Lysimachia clethroides

LYSIMACHIA
DISCO BALL

(continued)

(p. **103**)
SUMMER

ingredients section on right:

Secateurs/snips

String or twine –
I use butcher's twine

90cm length of
5cm gauge chicken wire

Strong 3mm binding wire,
enough to wrap around
the ball several times.

Mossing pins

Clear fishing wire

Floral foam sphere –
I've used 20cm
but you can get many sizes

10 Hydrangea heads

20 stems white Larkspur
Consolida ajacis

20 *Gaura lindheimerei* heads

20 stems white Lysimachia –
Veronica would work
just as well

5 Great Burnet
Sanguisorba officinalis stems

15 *Ammi majus* heads

1. Prepare the floral foam ball by dropping it gently into a deep bucket/sink of water. Don't push it down, just leave it to absorb water in its own time and by the time it's fully submerged it'll be ready to use, which will take no more than 10 minutes

2. Meanwhile, remove all the foliage from the stems. Sort the conditioned stems (see page 174) into families and lay them out in front of you. Snip the hydrangeas into small florets, cutting the stems at a sharp angle to enable easy access into the floral foam.

3. Cut the chicken wire so that it will generously wrap around the oasis ball. Next, take the binding wire and wrap it through and around the chicken wire-wrapped ball. Twist it together tightly and make a loop – the weight of the ball will hang from here so it needs to be secure.

4. Starting with the hydrangea florets, loosely cover the whole ball. This is your base. Then fill in the spaces with the Ammi. When there is no more floral foam on show, add the rest of the flowers randomly, to cover the whole ball. Finishing up with the lightest, airy wisps of the Gaura.

5. When you have your base covered, if it's accessible and easy for you to work from, hang the ball where it's going to be on display. This will make it much easier in the long run as otherwise you're going to bash the wispier, long stems that are sticking out of the ball.

6. To keep the flowers looking fresh, spritz with water at least once a day.

7. This disco ball is still hanging in our house, nearly a year after I made it. It's dried beautifully and although it's no longer green and fresh, the faded look is almost as pleasing.

21

Sweet Peas

Sweet peas remind me of summers when I was little – hazy, blue days in the garden with my brothers while my parents would be weeding and mowing. You can, of course, now get commercially grown, ramrod-straight, perfectly formed, super-long sweet peas. An absolute vision, they are irritatingly expensive and don't smell anything like home-grown ones. The non-uniformity of home-grown varieties is much more interesting but sadly they don't last for nearly as long as their foreign cousins. Do try to buy local if you can though.

Whether you buy or grow your own, giving your sweet peas a deep drink for a couple of hours in a cool, dark room adds several days to their life. This is also a great trick if they look like they're wilting. Cut 2.5cm off the bottom of the stem and then let them have a big drink – their crisp pertness will return in a flash.

As gorgeous as a huge bunch looks, sweet peas are quite fragile and arranging them in smaller groupings makes them last longer; I don't think they like being all squished up against each other like sardines.

They come in practically every colour under the sun and have the most delicious scent. It's hard to choose a favourite but I do find myself being consistently pulled towards the very pale lilac ones. They always manage to lift an arrangement – with a coral peony and a Solomon's seal they feel so vibrant, almost electric.

The bedroom where the sweet peas were heading is beyond feminine. Belonging to my appropriately named friend Violet, the entire room is a shrine to all things violet, both in colour and eclectic content. So the arrangement needed to fit the mood with a mix of purple and white sweet peas. I dotted little light bulb vases around the bedroom and used clear fishing wire to hang up the dangling ones. If you can't get hold of light bulb vases, though they are becoming a little more mainstream now, any small hanging glass vessels would work just as well. Little jam jars are good – fix wire round their necks and hang the fishing wire from that.

ALSO KNOWN AS

Lathyrus odoratus
Vase life 5 days

Clematis

With their fantastic climbing abilities and their huge range of shapes and colours, clematis are extremely popular garden plants. They also have fine woody stems which is great for arranging but sadly their downfall is their annoyingly short stems.

The variety I've used here in the wreath is called 'Blue Pirouette'. It does grow beautifully in gardens but thankfully it's also commercially grown in Holland. The commercially grown stems are bred to be much taller and straighter. With its purplish-blue starry, open-faced flowers perched at the end with white stamens shining out, it's ideal for arrangements and bouquets. Both short or long stems would work here, the length isn't especially important. The fact that the stems are fine and strong, however, is important, as these are the perfect type of stem when working with floral foam.

(p. **108**)
SUMMER

ALSO KNOWN AS

....

Clematis 'Blue Pirouette'
Summer wreath lasts
up to 2 weeks

Keep the flowers alive for longer by dropping the wreath gently into a sink of water and letting it have a drink for a few minutes every day. Drain properly before you reposition again.

CLEMATIS

(continued)

ingredients.

1. When working with floral foam, I like to create a wild and natural feel with the flowers to counteract the synthetic nature of the foam. It isn't hard to do this, simply vary the lengths of the flowers in the wreath so some are longer than others, and don't make the whole thing too methodical and neat. The other tip is not to cram in too many flowers as you don't want to make it look tidy and compact. Let the flowers breathe a bit, give them room to open and move around if they need to. Rosebuds for example will start off tiny but after a day or so when they open up they will want more space to breathe.

2. Start by soaking your floral foam heart by placing it in a large sink or bowl of water. Wait about 10 minutes until the water is fully absorbed, don't be tempted to poke it.

3. While you're waiting, condition your flowers (see page 174) and lay them out in front of you in families. You're going to be using fairly short lengths for this wreath so start by cutting them down to the size you want. Mine varied in size from about 10–20cm. I like to see some leaves on the clematis so don't remove them all, leave a couple nearest the clematis head, removing the ones lower down the stem.

4. When working with floral foam, you need to cut stems at an angle. This makes it easier to insert them in the foam and gives the flowers a bigger surface area to drink from.

5. When all your flowers are prepared, start by covering the base of the heart with a mix of the eucalyptus varieties until the whole heart is loosely covered. Next add the Pittosporum into the gaps.

6. I was taught that when using a foam base, a good guide is to add enough foliage so that the form looks as if it could be finished before adding flowers; you don't want to see any gaps but nor do you want it too tight. When you have full foliage coverage, start your flower ingredients by adding the roses. Do include the buds if there are any.

7. Next, add the clematis, and lastly, the waxflower. When making any wreath like this, saving the smallest flower until the end means you can work your way round, popping it into any obvious gaps.

8. A wreath doesn't have to always be hung – think about having one as a table centrepiece with a candle-lit glass hurricane lamp in the middle.

1 floral foam
heart wreath form

Snips/secateurs

6 stems *Eucalyptus cinerea*

6 stems *Eucalyptus pulverulenta*
'Baby Blue'

6 stems *Eucalyptus parvifolia*

(Don't worry too much if you
can't get the different varieties
of eucalyptus, a mixed bunch
works just as well.)

6 stems
Pittosporum tenuifolium

10 stems cream
Majolica spray roses

25 stems Clematis
'Blue Pirouette'
(You could use similar
garden varieties such as
Clematis *alpina* or
'Frances Rivis')

5 stems white
Waxflower *Chamelaucium*

(p. **111**)
SUMMER

23

Delphiniums

Delphiniums are kings of the cut flower kingdom. Standing tall and proud above their peers – they can reach over 2m tall – they are an absolute joy to use in big arrangements. They are my fail-safe for summer events. There was a real delphinium drought one year and my supplier sent me some rather weedy ones for a wedding I was doing – they were far more like their skimpier sister, the larkspur. I was so convinced that my input for the wedding would flop without them that I spent nine hours driving around the country to florists and green-fingered-friends begging them for a delphinium or two.

Delphiniums come in a range of blues, pinks and purples and a scintillating white. My favourites are the hybrid varieties that have dark brown 'eyes' and double flowers. Look out for the bright white and black 'Atholl', sky blue 'Langdon's Pandora' and sugary lilac 'Summerfield Miranda'. Delphiniums are perfect for mixing with other flowers, as in this arrangement, but they also look incredibly dramatic displayed by themselves either as a mixed colour arrangement or all one colour in a lovely big jug. It is a bit of a waste to cut them down for smaller arrangements as their scale is part of what makes them so striking, but many delphinium varieties have side-sprouting stems with tiny bellflowers and these look divine in smaller arrangements. You could use these on tables for a wedding or party. Simply snip them off the main stem and keep to one side in a jar of water until you need them.

(p. 115)
SUMMER

ALSO KNOWN AS

Delphinium elatum
Delphinium grandiflorum
Vase life 5–7 days

DELPHINIUMS

(continued)

1. Sort your conditioned flowers (see page 174) in front of you in families.

2. This arrangement is huge so it is best to take the container to where it's going to be on display and work on it in situ.

3. Soak the floral foam blocks in water for at least 10 minutes and assemble them in the container. The zinc planter I've used here is enormous so rather than using huge amounts of floral foam, I've filled the bottom with upturned crates and plastic plant pots and then put the wet floral foam on top. Make sure that it's firm and secure by cramming the blocks in as tightly as you can – floral foam needs to be firm or the flowers will be unsteady.

4. Start by creating the skeleton of the arrangement by adding the foliage, in this case, the beech, eucalyptus, euphorbia and the stephanandra. I always add the tallest stems first. Keep stepping back, looking at the shape as a whole.

5. When using floral foam, it's important not to keep inserting and then pulling out the stems again. Once you put in a stem, it wants to stay put. You can't re-add a stem into a hole, so think carefully before you place anything, especially when adding the thicker stems.

6. Add the remaining flowers, generally following the rule that you add them in decreasing size order. Keep stepping away to look at what you're doing.

7. If you can, remember to spritz the flowers every day with water and check the foam. If it feels dry to the touch add more water – never let it dry out otherwise the flowers will wilt.

---

ingredients.

Zinc planter – or any large planter, use a liner if necessary

8 blocks of floral foam

Snips/secateurs

5 branches in beech leaf
Fagus sylvatica

5 stems acid-green
Euphorbia oblongata

3 tall Stephanandra branches
Stephanandra incisa

9 'Summer Skies' delphiniums (pale lilac with dark brown eyes)

9 'Dewi Boy' pale blue delphiniums (you can of course use any colour you prefer)

10 coral peonies 'Coral Charm' or 'Coral Sunset'

10 dark red peonies – 'Red Charm' or 'Karl Rosenfield'

15 stems dark reddish purple *Astrantia minor* 'Moulin Rouge'

9 bright green hydrangea *Hydrangea macrophylla*

TIPS

Remove all the foliage and side flowers to
ensure the tall delphinium spires last as
long as possible, keeping any side flowers
to use in smaller arrangements.

When buying, or picking from
the garden, make sure most of the
flowers are open if you want to display
them right away. They open from
the bottom upwards.

Queen of the British cut flower garden,
Sarah Raven, suggests filling delphinium
stems with water, covering the stem
with your thumb and then placing it
back under the water in the container
immediately. This ensures that the
flowers keep hydrated and don't flop
too soon.

24
Wild Clematis

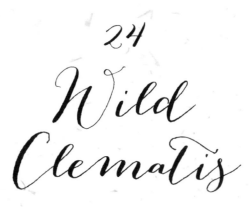

All the ingredients used to make this wreath were foraged. I'm not sure if I can use the word 'forage' if the items came from my garden but the wild clematis really *was* foraged: it came from a hedgerow near my house. In many countries, New Zealand for one, wild clematis is considered an out of control menace that needs to be reduced and controlled. So picking a small bit here and there is actually helpful. The hedgerows and woodlands in the British summer months are bursting with it. A vigorous climber, its leaf stalks cling to anything they come into contact with. And unless it is cut back, which helpfully rejuvenates the growth, mature clematis can climb to 12 metres.

The base of the wreath is made with grapevine offcuts. As the one in my garden needs pruning every winter it luckily provides me with a fresh supply for wreaths. But if you don't have vines, pliable willow or red or yellow dogwood (cornus) work just as well. Or if none of those suggestions can be found, then florists, garden centres and many online retailers all sell plain wreath bases.

Being without water, this won't last much more than 24 hours. Think about making it for a lunch or late summer party and hang it on a door or garden gate to welcome your guests.

(p. **116**)
SUMMER

ALSO KNOWN AS

Clematis vitalba
Traveller's Joy
Wreath life 2 days

To keep this arrangement going as long as possible,
mist with water every few hours.

WILD CLEMATIS

(continued)

ingredients.

10–15 vines or freshly cut
stems of willow (salix) or
dogwood (cornus),
about 1m long

5–10 long stems of clematis,
about 1.5m long

Reel wire

Snips/secateurs

15 *Ammi majus* heads

1. Take a couple of the vines or cut stems of willow or cornus and bend them together to form a circle. My wreath diameter was about 60cm so aim for this when making your base. Introduce another cut stem once you've made the initial circular shape, weaving it in and out to make the circle stronger.

2. Keep turning the circle. Starting at a different spot each time you poke in another stem, carry on until it reaches your desired thickness.

3. When you have a substantial base, take one of your clematis strands, poke it through the vines and weave it in and out as much as you can. You might want to use florist's wire here to secure it to the wreath base.

4. Continue until you have covered the wreath. How much you add is a matter of personal taste but I used about five strands. I like seeing a bit of the base underneath which makes it feel more airy and relaxed.

5. When you come across a really pretty, starry bit of clematis, don't be afraid to snip off bits and just slot them into the wreath. I love it looking haphazard and wild. It's not meant to be neat and perfect in any way.

Autumn

25
Japanese Anemones

I think these could be my favourite flowers. We've only been acquainted for a few years, yet no other flower manages to make me *quite* as happy as a Japanese anemone. They are a real dream. Standing tall on spaghetti-thin stems with their delicate cupped petals in the prettiest pinks, they remind me of ballerinas. Floating above serrated leaves, their gobstopper buds give a robust edge and stop them feeling too pretty.

Flowering in the garden from late summer to early autumn, some are more special than others. I adore the intensely white, single flowered *Anemone x hybrida* 'Honorine Jobert' with her golden stamens and luminous petals, but my absolute favourite is the rich pink 'Bressingham Glow' with her semi-double flowers and quilled petals. Pure unabashed prettiness.

With fiery orange walls and a hot pink fireplace, simple seemed to be the best flower option here. Using vintage ceramic condiment pots found on my travels, I simply filled them with armfuls of *A.hupehensis* 'Hadspen Abundance'. Keeping lots of the foliage – for bulk as much as the look – and also the buds, they look wild and full of character, like a crazy still life.

Japanese anemones don't last very long in the vase, on average about five days and if you keep a lot of the leaves on the stems they will wilt faster, so you need to make a choice between the look and how long they last. The more leaves you remove, the longer the display will last.

[p. **123**]
AUTUMN

ALSO KNOWN AS

Anemone hupehensis
and *A. x hybrida*
Vase life 5 days

26

Umbrella Fern

Ferns have been around for an unimaginably long time, which gives them a rather mystical wizardly air. Among the most complex of all the non-flowering plants, botanists believe they could have been in existence over 350 million years ago.

I'm growing to appreciate ferns. Lovely as plants in the wild, the cut stems are trickier to mix into flower arrangements. This isn't really for any reason other than personal taste. If they're going to come inside as they are here, I prefer to let them speak for themselves on a solo mission.

These are umbrella ferns, native to Australia, and they really do look like frilly umbrellas or miniature palm trees. Their soft, frilly fronds appear delicate and fragile but are actually very hardy and long lasting – perfect for creating displays.

This arrangement is supposed to have a lush, tropical feel. The ferns would also look amazing dotted down a big, long table in varying heights on a balmy summery evening.

(p. 127)
AUTUMN

ALSO KNOWN AS

Sticherus flabellatus
Vase life up to 2 weeks

UMBRELLA FERN

(continued)

(p. **128**)
AUTUMN

ingredients.

Snips/secateurs

Floral foam balls – about 10cm

Pot tape

2 large wooden candleholders –
mine were 70cm tall

20 umbrella ferns *Sticherus
flabellatus*

20 eucalyptus stems

1. These are super simple to make. If you don't have floral foam balls, cut off 2 small chunks from a big floral foam brick, about 10cm x 10cm each and drop them into a bucket of water. Wait for them to fully absorb, it'll take no more than 10 minutes. Don't push them down to hurry them along as this will create airpockets. When the floral foam is fully soaked – it will be a uniform darker green colour – using the pot tape, secure each ball to the top of the candlesticks.

2. Now for the fun bit. Start inserting the umbrella ferns, one by one. You will need to trim the stalks quite short, mine were about 10cm. Try and do this bit in situ, where they're going to be displayed if possible.

3. Keep covering the floral foam with the ferns, remembering to step back and look at what you're doing – the distance will give you a better idea of the shape you're creating. You're aiming for a palm tree/circular shape.

4. When you've run out of ferns, fill in any gaps with the eucalyptus stems. I like these to be rather long and wayward – the crazier they are I find the more character they have.

5. I wanted these to be purely green but there's no reason why you couldn't add some flowers to the mix. I was quite tempted to add some miniature pineapples.

6. To prolong their life, mist daily with water, they should then last up to two weeks.

27
Apple Branches

There's something slightly decadent about using fruit in flower arrangements. An incredible American florist called Ariella Chezar is responsible for inspiring my own fruit-filled creations and I especially love her use of kumquats and vine tomatoes.

This apple display here is ridiculously simple but at the same time eye-catching and dramatic. It would make a great alternative to flowers if budgets were tight for a wedding or party. I've just used one type of apple but a mix, including some much smaller crab apples, would look great for a bit of variety and to introduce another colour. 'Golden Hornet' crab apple would be a very sunny yellow addition.

I've used a stripy container as a vase. It's an old Wade Royal Victoria pottery barrel that was once filled with sherry. Being an old keg, it's got a massive hole at the bottom so I made a liner using a large yogurt pot, which I inserted and filled with water. Large decorative olive oil cans also make wonderful containers for something as simple but as stunning as an apple arrangement.

(p. 130)
AUTUMN

ALSO KNOWN AS

Malus
Vase life 2 weeks

Mixing types, colours and sizes of apples also looks
very effective. Great for autumnal weddings.

28
Old Man's Beard

When clematis has finished flowering, the developing seeds hold on to an element of the flower, called the style. This has long, silky, grey hairs, which form little cotton woolly, wispy balls, resembling old men's beards, hence the name. As well as looking fab, the silky hairs also have a purpose, which is to disperse the seeds.

Old man's beard isn't especially pretty in itself, but for decorating it can be dreamy. Being a climbing vine, it behaves perfectly in wreaths and garlands and it makes life so easy as it literally *wants* to wrap itself around things. It's great for its longevity too, you can keep this wreath up for months, adding a changing cast of fresh flowers if you want to. One word of warning though, it can be quite tricky to disentangle and you will need patience if you're wanting long swathes of it.

To make this wreath, follow the instructions on page 119 for the flowering clematis version but swap it for old man's beard instead at the last stage.

This wreath is about 45cm wide. You can, of course, make it any size to suit your taste. I once made an enormous one, about 1 metre wide and it hung in our hallway for over a year. I only took it down because the silky strands had been completely replaced with dust.

ALSO KNOWN AS

Clematis vitalba
Traveller's Joy
Wreath life 6 months

ALSO KNOWN AS

....

Dahlia hortensis varieties

Vase life 4 days

29

Dahlias

If spring is for peonies and summer is for roses, dahlias have early autumn all sewn up. This is when they are at their prime. In the most incredible colours, in so many forms and sizes, with wonderfully crazy names, they are a gift. I am completely mad about them and can't quite get over the fact that when we got married in September 2008, my mother did all the flowers and I had such a dislike of dahlias that I banned her from using them anywhere at our wedding. If we were to marry now, they would practically be *all* I would use. They do have a slight reputation for being 'Granny flowers' and they're not all equally lovely, but there are so many that are mesmerisingly beautiful. There are also some that are so gaudy and so loud that they fit into a 'so bad they're good' category.

Come autumn, my studio is full of visions grown by the amazing Bridget Elworthy from the Land Gardeners. She has the best taste and the best quality plants and I now plan my arrangements for people around what she has in stock. She's introduced me to my two favourite dahlias – 'Santa Claus', which is striped orange and white and a rich purple called 'Thomas A. Edison'.

Sometimes I do struggle to know what to do with dahlias, whether to mix them up with other flowers and foliage or allow them to show off their beauty all by themselves (I have this issue with peonies too). Here I've let them take centre stage. I've chosen a mix of crazy favourites and displayed them in a rather loud, vintage tea set I found in an antiques market in France. Personally I think this whole arrangement falls into the 'so bad it's good' category and the bright cheeriness of it all makes me so happy. It's definitely not for any shrinking violet, minimalists out there! Display-wise, you can treat dahlias like specimens and dot down a mantelpiece or kitchen table in test tubes and scientific containers where people can examine and admire them. They can look very dramatic like this, especially if you have a very long table and an abundance of flowers. ➤

DAHLIAS

(continued)

Dahlias originate in Mexico and even though there are thousands of varieties now, they all descend from just 30 original species. Unlike most plants which possess just two chromosomes, dahlias have eight, which over the years clever hybridisers have been able to exploit, and is the reason for all the new and exciting forms that keep popping up all over the place. Dahlias don't behave especially well as cut flowers, their shelf life is only about 3–4 days and many do drop their petals too soon, but as long as you know this and plan accordingly they are the most magical addition to any arrangement. As enchanting as the huge, dinner plate varieties are, the smaller ones are much easier to arrange and work better alongside other flowers. Think about keeping the larger ones for stand-alone displays.

SOME FAVOURITES

Dahlias come in all different forms and sizes, from spiky cacti to soft pom poms, huge decorative discs to the more fragile, single-petal tree peony types. With the exception of 'Café au Lait', an enormous, pale pinky-cream decorative dahlia used a lot in weddings, my favourites are always the crazy ones, the ones that you can't quite believe are real. The orange and white striped 'Santa Claus', the purple tipped 'Tartan' and the speckled pink 'Blackberry Ripple' are my best showstoppers.

There's obviously not a lot of arranging going on in this display, it's more about the mix of colours and shapes and quite a personal thing. However, a fail-safe arrangement that I've created for a few events, and which works for any occasion – wedding, funeral or a party – is a mix of 'Santa Claus' with rich, glossy purple 'Tomo' plus lots of small, pale and bright blue delphiniums, lime green *Alchemilla mollis* and plenty of wayward beech leaf. It's very wild, colourful, seasonal and eye-catching, a dream combo.

TIPS

Plunge into water up to their necks
and leave overnight in a dark room
before using.

Ideally, dahlias like warm water –
the warmth moves the water and
nutrients more quickly into the
stems than cold water.

Remove any foliage that falls
under the water line.

Trim the stems under water
to prevent air blocks.

Change the water if you notice it
becoming cloudy.

Winter

30
Pink Jasmine Kokedama

Don't be confused by the 'pink' in the name as jasmine's small starry petals are as white as white can be. Pink refers to the rosy tinted buds before flowering.

Along with hellebores, narcissi and hyacinths, jasmine is a gorgeous houseplant to live with while you wait for the spring flowers to wake up outside. And it has the most delicious, intense scent. It reminds me so much of when I was little, when jasmine climbed our greenhouse walls and my brothers and I used to spend hours methodically pulling off the little white heads to suck out droplets of (probably imaginary) nectar.

Jasmine likes to be kept in a cool, well-lit, bright (but out of direct sunlight) room. If it's too hot or too dark, the white petals will turn brown. A cool bathroom makes a good home while the buds are developing as they like humidity. Never let the compost dry out but never saturate the soil either. Misting the compost with a water spritzer every few days works well.

I've turned this jasmine plant into a *kokedama* or moss ball. In a nutshell, it's a Japanese practice where you remove a plant from its container and gently get rid of the soil surrounding the roots. Then the roots are wrapped in a ball of special compost, covered in moss and wrapped up again in twine to make a ball. People outside Japan have recently gone crazy for these and have created whole hanging 'string gardens' with them. This one's not actually hanging but the suspended ones are a great idea if you are low on space, they're perfect for confined city living. You can 'kokedamise' almost any plant – for inspiration have a look at the creations made by the modern day king of *kokedama* Netherlands-based Fedor van der Valk.

(p. 143)
WINTER

PINK JASMINE
KOKEDAMA

(continued)

ingredients.

Gardening gloves

A small jasmine plant. If you can't get hold of jasmine or want to try a different plant, choose something that likes shade as moss doesn't like direct sunlight. Ferns would be a great option.

A mix of garden soil, peat-free compost and some garden grit for drainage – you're aiming for a clay-like consistency.

Water

Dry sphagnum moss

Reel of cotton string

Ball of brown twine, hemp or sisal string

1. Remove your plant from its container and very gently remove all the soil that surrounds the roots.

2. Mix the garden and akedama soil together, forming a ball big enough to hold your plant in the middle. You might want to add water to get the right consistency. You'll know you've got this right when the soil holds together nicely without crumbling apart. Put it to one side.

3. Now take the dry sphagnum moss and wrap it around the exposed roots forming a neat, compact ball shape. Tie the cotton string around this ball shape you've just created. This will hold it together for now but will eventually dissolve.

4. Now, come back to your soil ball, make a hole in the middle and very gently, push in the plant, making sure you secure it properly by smoothing it with your hands back into a sphere shape.

5. When it is rounded and compact, start covering up the soil by pushing in little bits of the sphagnum moss into the soil.

6. Finish off with your twine by wrapping it round and round the ball, to hold it all together. Leave a long thread if you want to hang your ball. Either way, find a shady, cool place to display the beauty.

7. Mist every day with a water sprayer or alternatively, drop into a sink of water once a week for a few minutes and if you are hanging it let it drip dry somewhere before re-hanging.

31
Miniature Pineapples

These are not a flower but I feel they are close enough and I really wanted to include them, so please forgive me for slipping a fruit into a flower book. People can't get enough of these when I use them at events. For the amount of excitement they bring about, you'd be forgiven for thinking it was George Clooney on the table rather than a lot of very tiny pineapples.

Miniature pineapples are grown in Brazil, more as ornamental novelties than for a plentiful fruit crop. They arrive on very long stems which means they can be used as 'flowers' in arrangements or they can be cut free from their stems and used as candlestick extensions. They are also very happy to be sprayed gold, or any other colour. Think about using them as placement card holders for each dinner party guest, or mixing them in with full-size pineapples and dotting them down a table, weaving in between jugs of flowers.

To keep the pineapples upright, you might need to slice their bottoms off to give you a flat surface. Sometimes, the candles don't seem to want to sit still either, but a bit of Blu-Tack on the base of the candle will rectify this in no time.

Another joy of these miniature creations is how long they last – I've had some that are still on the stems and last for weeks and weeks in water. Out of water, cut off their stems and you'll still get at least two weeks out of them before they start to crinkle up a bit.

(p. 146)
WINTER

ALSO KNOWN AS

Ananas bracteatus

Red pineapple

Arrangement life –

1 month in water;

1 week out of water

Dinner party line-up; change the candle colour to fit
in with your theme.

32

Hellebores

I've developed rather a short fuse with cut hellebores after one too many wilting disasters so now I've moved on to using them in plant form. Cut hellebores are very temperamental and need to be picked at exactly the right point or they flop. Fine(ish) if you're playing around at home with them but if they're for an event it's just too risky. I did a friend's birthday party one Christmas, I set it all up in the morning and left it looking ravishing. Coming back five hours later, everything was great bar the hellebores, which were having the worst time ever and had all taken a nosedive. Disastrous. I spent the whole evening unable to focus on anything other than my floral failings. So, for now at least, I'm sticking to plants, which are far more amenable and last ten times as long. If you're feeling brave though and want to give it a go, dip the bottom of the stems in just boiled water for 20–30 seconds and then leave them in water up to their necks overnight, to give you the best chance of survival. You never want flowerheads to be touched by steam so keep them out of the way by gently wrapping the heads in newspaper.

I remember these swan vases being around when I was little. I thought they were hideous then, and actually I still do, but there's something retro and serene about them, even more so when there's a whole flotilla of them swanning around. These plants are particularly beautiful with such luminous white petals and stunning starry yellow centres. There's something impressively majestic about them.

Hellebores, some of which are also known as Christmas roses, make great indoor plants. They traditionally bloom from midwinter, but hothouse forcing means they now appear in the markets and garden centres right at the start of winter, if not before. While not exactly festive in the way of holly or ivy, they are a wonderful addition to your winter flower wardrobe, and equally cheering in the gloomy days of late winter.

ALSO KNOWN AS

Helleborus niger,
Helleborus orientalis
Christmas rose, Lenten rose
Vase life up to 1 month

HELLEBORES

(continued)

ingredients.

....

Ceramic swan vases

**As many hellebores
(*Helleborus niger*) plants
as you have pots**

A few large handfuls of moss

1. To repot the hellebores into the swans is very simple. Gently prise them out of their plastic pots and drop them into their new home. If their pots happen to sit perfectly in the swan you could leave them in it as this makes watering much easier.

2. If the plant is slightly too big, gently shake off enough of the soil until it fits, and finish off by covering the top of the soil with moss.

3. Keep them well watered, out of full sun and not too warm and they should flower into early spring and even beyond. When they've finished flowering you can plant them outside in any slightly shady, damp spot in the garden and they should come back to life again the following year.

ALSO KNOWN AS

Orchidaceae
Available all year round
Lasts for 8 weeks

33

Orchids

There are so many different types of orchid – about 30,000 in the wild and then at least 120,000 man-made hybrids at the last count. *Orchidaceae*, along with *Asteraceae*, are the two largest flowering plant families on the planet.

I used to be rather dismissive of orchids. I decided they were not my style, a bit too tropical, too everywhere, too obvious. But now, the more I work with flowers, the more I'm beginning to enjoy them. There are some real beauties out there that I never even thought were orchids. If you mix them in with very wild, country-style flowers and foliage there's scarcely a whiff of the tropics, more a feeling of lux. It's all about the balance.

Saying that, the orchids used here *are* pretty tropical, but they are lovely being so small. So much better than their shoutier relatives that you find in supermarkets and garden centres. They also work really well contained like this in old pickle jars – a kind of a terrarium. It makes them feel like exotic specimens. My sons adore them like this too and are actually 'looking after them' for me in their bedrooms. Keeping orchids is a great way of introducing children to gardening and flowers.

Most orchid species grow in rainforests where they like the humidity and the shade. Housing them in glass helps mimic that environment while the open top lets the air circulate freely.

A lot of people struggle to keep orchids alive and it's often looking after them *too* much that kills them. Too much water is a killer. Literally. Give them one pudding spoon of water a week, always from the top and allow it to drain through. Never let the pot stand in water for a long time. Mist the foliage every three days to keep up the humidity levels.

(p. 155)
WINTER

ORCHID

(continued)

Mini orchids. These are mini purple Phalaenopsis. There are so many beautiful miniature orchids, my favourite is *Ornithophora radicans*.

Large recycled glass jar

Pincushion moss – this can be found in the woods if you live in the countryside, otherwise from a florist

Lichen if available

1. Start by taking your orchid out of its container and gently remove all the soil from the roots. Orchids are air plants, they don't actually *need* soil.

2. Next add the clumps of moss. Ideally use pincushion moss as the little smooth chunks are far prettier that its flatter, more murky-coloured cousin.

3. Then nestle the orchid plant in between the moss balls, making it as secure as you can. Use the moss as support for the orchid.

4. The lichen is just for decoration, just scatter it on top of the moss. The purer the air, the more lichen you may find, keep your eyes peeled for it when you go for country or woodland walks. In the UK, Wales and Cornwall are major lichen hotspots.

34
Paperwhite Narcissi

(p. **160**)
WINTER

Paperwhite narcissi belong to the daffodil family and, in my opinion, reign supreme over their whole kingdom. Their sparkling white, delicate petals and heavenly scent bring huge joy to a quiet time of year on the flower front. As well as using them as potted bulbs as in this arrangement, they are just as gorgeous and easy to source as cut flowers too. Along with muscari (grape hyacinth) and amaryllis, paperwhites are some of the easiest bulbs to grow for indoor displays at home, they usually take six weeks from planting to flower.

I've used an enormous piece of cork tree bark as the container here. When I lived in France I used to find coracle-like shards of it on the ground and would drag them home as woodland treasure. It gives a fantastically wild and rustic look. As well as using them as planters they also make great plates – perfect for substantial crudité platters.

For a stunning festive arrangement with narcissi as cut flowers rather than bulbs, you can mix them with white ranunculus, dusty miller *Centaurea cineraria*, acid green bupleurum and magnolia buds. Lots of small vases dotted down the table both look and smell incredible.

ALSO KNOWN AS

Narcissi

Vase life 2 weeks in

cool conditions

PAPERWHITE
NARCISSI

(continued)

ingredients.

30 Paperwhite bulbs –
or as many as you can
fit in your container
(don't skimp on quantities)

Compost

Gravel/small stones

10 twigs from the garden

Moss

Bark planter – If you can't
get bark like this, think about
using an old wooden wine box,
a huge china cachepot or
an old wicker basket, lined

1. Sprinkle the gravel or stones into the bottom of the container.
   These will act as drainage.

2. Add a layer of soil about 10cm deep on top of the gravel and
   drop the bulbs in, leaving about 2cm between each one. Cover
   with another 2cm of soil, not too much, give them a good
   drink and let them drain.

3. They then want to sit in a cool dark room for 7–10 days to
   stimulate the roots. As soon as they start sprouting, bring
   them out into the light. Rotate the container every few days
   to keep the stalks straight.

4. When they are ready to face their public, cover the topsoil
   with moss and stake with some twiggy branches picked from
   the garden. These will act as supports when the flower stems
   get taller and more wayward. I love using hazel or, for a real
   winter wonderland feel, I spray the twigs white.

5. Remember to water them every few days and to ensure the
   flowers bloom for as long as possible, keep them cool and away
   from direct sunlight.

6. Think about staggering the planting times to give you a long
   succession of flowers. It's rather sad when they all bloom and
   wilt at the same time – although keeping them in the cold does
   postpone their moment of glory.

7. When daffodils and narcissi stems are first cut, they produce
   a toxic sap. Unlike some other flowers, they can't be cauterised.
   To stop the sap flow, stand them in water for an hour by
   themselves and then arrange in fresh water.

35

Amaryllis

Amaryllis is a show-off flower that likes to be centre stage, definitely not a shy retiring type that can merge into the background. They are exotic and tropical looking, almost like updated lilies with their velvety trumpet flowers perched on top of such stately stems. Until recently I felt that cutting them down in size was almost a sin but I'm learning that they can be just as magnificent with slightly shorter stems.

Synonymous with the holidays and Christmas they are wonderful for creating mega, show-stopping festive arrangements. My Christmas events always include majestic deep red 'Royal Velvet' and 'Tinto Night', but I also love the bi-colour varieties, especially 'Green Magic' with its soft green petals flecked with crimson feathering.

(p. **164**)
WINTER

Despite their festive connotations, amaryllis are actually available all year round, and they come in so many irresistible colours, from burgundy to coral, crimson to lime green stripes, that there's a flower for every colour theme. I'm not sure if I prefer them as planted bulbs or cut stems in a vase. The bulbs last for so much longer but obviously need forward planning – allow six weeks from planting the bulb to the trumpet's opening.

I struggle to think of another cut flower that has the commanding pizzazz and regal presence of an amaryllis. Saying that, their size is not for everyone, or every occasion. They demand a great deal of space and the stems are so thick they need a generous container with a wide bottom and narrow neck to give both space and support – I love them in a vintage pickle jar. ➛

ALSO KNOWN AS

Hippeastrum

Vase life 7–14 days

AMARYLLIS
(continued)

Another drawback is that their succulent hollow stems and top heavy heads make amaryllis prone to snapping. It's worth inserting fine wooden canes (from a garden centre) inside the stems to make them sturdier. To insert a cane lay the amaryllis on a table with the head hanging off the side. Taking care not to bash the delicate petals, insert a cane the full length of the stem very slowly and carefully into the stem until just below the head – you'll feel it jam. This will make them last up to 14 days without snapping. The bottoms of amaryllis stems can split and start curling upwards so if they are visible in your container either trim the stems every day or wrap the bases with waterproof tape to prevent them splitting.

For a very simple but dramatic large-scale arrangement, mix five or six amaryllis with the same number of hydrangeas and lots of wayward eucalyptus branches. They will last in a vase for up to three weeks if you keep the water topped up and fresh. Changing the water in large arrangements can be a rather tricky process so unless you can remove the flowers easily to tip out the water and start again, I'd suggest simply adding a bit of fresh water to the arrangement every other day.

36

Eucalyptus

If I could use only one type of foliage in the winter, eucalyptus would be my top choice. Although, once I've dismantled all my garlands and wreaths at Christmas, I'm happy to say goodbye to it for another year. But saying that, it is the most amenable, aromatic plant that can transform your home into a scented winter wonderland, just by bringing it through the front door.

In arrangements, its elegant grey foliage is a perfect foil for amaryllis or roses, but most of all it can elevate garlands and wreaths into something special. The fact that it can last without water makes it especially valuable too. Inevitably it does dry up but still looks and smells good. I do rather like this crispiness, although it will stay softer if you mist the leaves daily with a water spray. For me, the best thing about eucalyptus is the pungent menthol scent that comes from the aromatic oil in its silvery blue leaves. The scent seems to intensify as the leaves dry and smells far more delicious than an expensive winter scented candle. It's instantly calming and I haven't met anyone who dislikes it.

(p. **168**)
WINTER

The garland hanging from this mantelpiece is made with different varieties of eucalyptus. The tree is native to Australia, where it's known as gum tree, there are over 700 different species of eucalyptus. You can buy it in a useful range of lengths from long branches to stubbier sprigs with varying leaf sizes. Ideally, when making a garland, you want pliable, medium length boughs. The main leaf I've used is *Eucalyptus cinerea* or 'Silver Dollar' and the rest of the garland is made up with the seeded and baby blue varieties, berried ivy, spruce and then lots of dried hydrangeas to introduce a floral element.

This garland is very natural and tonal. The surroundings were rather opulent so I wanted something that would complement them rather than compete. It goes without saying that, of course, you can add anything you like to the garland if you want to up the wow factor. I thought about echoing the gold surrounding by adding gilded Peruvian peppercorns but changed my mind at the last minute. It suddenly felt a bit too blingy.

ALSO KNOWN AS

....

Gum tree, Argyle apple,
Silver dollar
Vase life 4 weeks in water
Out of water it will crisp up
after a couple of days.

EUCALYPTUS
(continued)

ingredients.

String or ribbon

Reel wire

Snips/secateurs

3 bunches of *Eucalyptus cinerea*

1 bunch of berried eucalyptus

1 bunch of *Eucalyptus pulverulenta* 'Baby Blue'

1 spruce garland base

20 stems of berried ivy

15–20 dried hydrangeas

1. Start by measuring how long you want the garland to be, using some string or ribbon, and then add 20cm to each end to use as the hanging loops.

2. Lay the string or ribbon out on the floor and then add the foliage on top of it.

3. You basically want to make a foliage sausage. The fatter the better.

4. Next, take the reel wire and, starting at one end, carefully wrap the foliage to the string or ribbon, binding up and around the sausage to hold it all together. Don't panic if it looks a bit stiff and solid at this stage.

5. Personally, I prefer to hang the garland in situ at this stage. I find it easier to see what I'm doing and if you fill it properly and *then* move it, there's likely to be quite a lot of fall whilst in transit.

6. Either way you choose to do it, add enough foliage until the garland looks full enough that you could happily display it as is. So make it full, and bushy, please. Then start feeding in the flowers.

37

Magnolia

I adore magnolia flowers, especially the frilly, starry petalled *Magnolia stellata*, but the buds of all varieties are also lovely. They look gorgeous mixed into arrangements with other flowers and, equally, hanging out in a solo role as they are here. The branches themselves are rather architectural, deep brown with tough, geometric stems jutting out in all directions, then at their tips you discover the milky green, velveteen shoots that soften the feel completely.

    This arrangement was perfect for a winter party where we didn't have a huge budget. It couldn't be simpler to create, yet attracted so many compliments. What made this arrangement even better is that after a few weeks the flowers decided to come out. Sometimes the buds die and sadly *won't* flower. It's pretty obvious and easy to tell if they're alive or not; they lose their velvety sheen then turn black and dry. Just gently prise these off and the rest of the buds should continue to flower. Keep water levels topped up and change the water if it starts to look murky.

(p. 172)
WINTER

ALSO KNOWN AS

Magnolia grandiflora
Southern magnolia, Bull Bay
Vase life 2–3 weeks

ingredients.

····································

1 large glass vase or any
other sizeable container

10 *Magnolia grandiflora* stems

25 gold Christmas baubles
You can of course use
anything you like to hang off
them. Our theme was disco
so these were perfect for us.

CONDITIONING

I have been writing a *lot* about 'conditioning'.
This is basically just preparing your flowers as well
as you can to ensure they last as long as possible.

1. Remove any unnecessary foliage, especially any bits that lie under the water line. Leaves left in the water will create a lot of bacteria, turning the water a horrible sludgy colour. Removing foliage also ensures that the water goes to the flowers rather than the leaves.

2. Flowers bought from a florist should come conditioned. When you get them home, re-cut about 1cm from the end of the stems and give them a drink for about an hour before arranging, if you can. Always cut stems on a diagonal with secateurs, flower snips or a sharp knife.

3. Imported flowers will have been picked and then immediately packaged – they won't have been conditioned at all. Snip the ends off, remove all leaves that will lie under the water line and give them a nice long, cool drink for an hour or so before arranging.

4. For home-grown and foraged flowers, remove all unwanted leaves, snip the ends and give a long cool drink for as long as possible before arranging, preferably for more than an hour. When you are picking your own flowers, get them into water as soon as you can. Ideally, pick in the early morning, never in the heat of the sun. If you can, put them in a bucket of lukewarm water, in the dark, plunged up to their necks, overnight. This will give them the best start.

5. Condition hollow-stemmed flowers like delphiniums, amaryllis and lupins by turning them upside down, filling the stem with water and then plugging with cotton wool. If you don't have cotton wool, keep your thumb over the end and don't let go until the stem is under the water.

6. In the past people have suggested bashing or hammering woody stems – lilac, Guelder rose and roses for example – but current thinking is that this may do more harm than good as it may increase the rate of bacterial infection and also damage the vascular system of the branch, restricting water intake.

....

7 . I make a vertical cut of about 5cm upwards from the base of woody stems – particularly garden roses.

8 . Flowers that are prone to droop, such as hellebores, euphorbia and poppies, can be seared before arranging. Dip the end of the stems, about 2cm or 10 per cent of the length of the flower, into very hot water (just off the boil). Be careful to keep the steam away from the petals, either cup your hands round them or wrap them carefully in newspaper.

9 . If roses droop they can be revived by re-cutting the ends of the stems and searing in the same way as above.

10 . Be very careful when handling euphorbia. It has a toxic sap so wear gloves and avoid getting it in your eyes at all costs. You can sear the end of the stem by holding it over a flame to cauterise it and stop the sap flowing.

11 . My favourite tip for reviving hydrangeas is to plunge them headfirst into a bucket of water and leave for as long as possible. Overnight is ideal.

12 . Peonies are very thirsty creatures and will need their vase water topped up every day. To condition them, float them in deep water overnight. They can drink from their petals so the more of the flower that's in contact with the water, the better. This should work to revive wilting ones too.

13 . Try not to place your cut flowers in direct sunlight, in a draught or near a heat source. They like to be kept in as cool a room as possible – unless they're tropical, like orchids, proteas and strelitzia, and then they prefer a little more warmth and humidity.

14 . One exception to the rule is if you are trying to force flowers to bloom. In that case sitting them near a radiator, a range cooker or in sunlight will work wonders.

GENERAL CARE
AND TIPS
FOR LONGEST
VASE LIFE

Keep things clean

Make sure your vases and containers are always clean. Any lurking
bacteria will shorten the life of your flowers. If you are able to put vases
in a dishwasher, do. For trickier vases to clean, add some bleach or
Milton sterilising tablets and clean with a baby bottle brush.

Water temperature

Using lukewarm rather than ice-cold water gives flowers more oxygen,
and this will keep them alive for longer.

Plant food

When you buy flowers from a florist they will give you a sachet of plant
food. If you're picking from your own garden and want to use some,
it's very easy to make your own.

To make one litre of the solution mix

1 litre water

1 tablespoon vinegar

1 teaspoon sugar

3–5 drops household bleach

———

Stir the water thoroughly before adding the flowers.

The bleach and vinegar reduce the chance of bacteria
multiplying. Bacteria cause stems to become slimy
and turn the water cloudy. The sugar acts as
food for the flowers.

TECHNIQUES

Using floral foam

1. Start by filling a bucket or sink with water and then drop in the foam. Don't let the foam run under a tap as this will cause air blocks inside that you won't be able to see and the stems will then wilt.

2. Allow the foam to take up the water naturally in its own time. No prodding. It will take no more than 10 minutes. When the foam is level with the surface of the water, fish it out and let it drain. Oversoaking will cause the foam to crumble.

3. For traditional arrangements, cut the foam so it is 2.5cm higher than the rim of the container, this will give a more natural feel. It lets you arrange flowers facing both upwards and down rather than just straight up.

4. When inserting stems, make sure you cut them on a diagonal. This gives the stems a bigger surface area to take up water and the point is easier to insert into foam.

5. Once you have inserted a stem, try not to pull it out and replace it. You shouldn't add stems into existing holes as it's likely you'll be left with an air pocket under the new stem, causing it to wilt.

6. When securing foam to a container, try and use the thinnest pot tape you can. There's nothing worse than not being able to add a stem somewhere because there's so much tape in the way. I use a tape that is about 0.5cm wide.

7. Floral foam is great for allowing you to create compositions that would otherwise be very difficult to support. You'd really struggle, for example, to make a disco ball without floral foam.

....

How to make a hand-tied bouquet

The key to making a good bouquet is to have a good variety of flowers – lots of different shapes, textures and sizes. Choose flowers with fine stems as this makes arranging easier. Aim for about five different types of flower.

Keep the flowers loose in your hand and you'll be able to move things up and down more easily. And you don't want to crush your stems. ➤

Also try and finish with the hardier stems on the outside – soft stems will be crushed by the string that holds it all together.

How to make a hand-tied bouquet

1. Condition your flowers and lay them out in families in front of you.

2. Choose a lead flower to begin with, something quite big like a rose, which will become the centre of the bouquet. Holding it in your left hand (if you are right-handed – swap if you're left-handed), add a few stems of foliage around it.

3. Each time you add a flower, lay it diagonally on top of the last then, with your free hand, turn the bunch. If you want to create a domed effect, keep adding the flowers slightly lower each time. Always turn in the same direction – this forms a spiral shape and makes it easy to add or remove any wayward stems. If the flowers you've chosen are particularly dainty, you might want to add more than one stem before turning.

4. Keep adding the flowers and remember to turn after each addition. Ideally you don't want the same flowers next to each other so keep track of what you are doing and hold the bouquet out in front of you every so often so you can look at the bouquet as a whole.

5. When you are happy with the shape and size of the bouquet, wrap a length of raffia or string around the top of the binding point, just above your hands, and tie in a knot to hold it all together.

6. Trim the ends of the stems straight across so that the bunch can stand upright in a vase and all the stems will be in water. The spiral formation means it will stand beautifully.

7. To sum up – take your main flower, twist, add foliage, twist, add a flower, twist, add foliage, twist…

....

How to make a garland

1. Start by measuring how long you want the garland to be, using some string or ribbon, and then add 20cm to each end to use as the hanging loops.

2. Lay the string or ribbon out on the floor and then add the foliage on top of it.

3. You basically want to make a foliage sausage, the fatter the better.

4. Next, take the reel wire and starting at one end, carefully wrap the foliage to the string or ribbon, binding up and around the sausage to hold it all together. Don't panic if it looks a bit stiff and solid at this stage.

5. Personally, I prefer to hang the garland in situ at this stage. I find it easier to see what I'm doing and also if you fill it properly and *then* move it, there's likely to be quite a lot of fall while in transit.

6. Either way you choose to do it, add enough foliage until the garland looks full enough that you could happily display it as is. So make it full, and bushy, please. Then start feeding in the flowers. In the eucalyptus garland I've made on page 168 the only flowers I used were dried hydrangeas. This is great to remember if budgets are tight, you really don't need buckets of flowers to create something mega. And you can always add in a few silk flowers.

7. The easiest way to hang a garland is to knock a couple of nails into each end of a fireplace (or wherever you want to hang the garland) and attach the garland to the nails with the wire you've used to wrap it with. Sometimes you won't be able to knock holes in things though, in which case I use removable hooks. Attach several of the removable hooks evenly spaced on top of the mantelpiece (or area you want to hang the garland). Using fishing wire, attach the garland to the hooks. If you can see the wire, disguise it by adding a new piece of eucalyptus or hydrangea.

TOOLKIT

If you are planning on playing around with flowers on a regular basis
or even thinking about creating some sort of flowery business,
it's a good idea to start building some sort of floral toolbox.

Cutting

When I was on a course at the Covent
Garden Academy of Flowers in London, they
introduced me to Japanese secateurs. They
were completely life-changing. I'm now spoiled
and can never use anything else! Other florists
prefer long-nosed snips or floral scissors for soft
stems and secateurs for woodier material. Try
them out in your hand before you buy any snips
as you'll be using them a lot. You'll find what
works for you.

Scissors

I try not to use my secateurs for anything other
than flowers. There's always lots of paper to
snip and elastics to cut away from huge wraps
of flowers.

Knives

A small, sharp knife is useful for removing
thorns from roses. You also need a larger knife
for cutting floral foam.

Mossing pins

These are U-shaped lengths of wire for holding
things in place when making wreaths and
working with floral foam. Originally designed
for keeping moss in place, they are also very
handy for securing foliage, flower heads, fruit,
ribbon, flowers with soft stems, fabric and bark.

Pot tape or anchor tape

An essential florist's tool for anchoring wet
floral foam to containers, and for securing
chicken wire forms into vases.

Stem tape

Waterproof green plastic covered tape, used
to bunch flowers together and to cover and seal
in the moisture of individually wired flowers
and stems.

Chicken wire/netting wire

For using in containers as a structure and to
keep stems in place.

Stub wire

Lengths of stub wire are used for wiring small
flowers for buttonholes and head crowns.
There are different gauges to use, depending on
the size of the flower. The smaller the gauge,
the thicker the wire.

Reel wire

I mostly use this when making garlands.
It comes in lots of different colours and
thicknesses and comes in one long length
on a roll.

Flower frogs/pin holders

These are small discs that can be made from
glass, lead, pottery or bronze. They sit at the
bottom of a vase or container to hold flower
arrangements in place. There are spiky ones to
hold thin and flimsy flowers, ones with holes
for thicker stems like tulips and hairpin frogs
with wire loops for woody stems and branches.
They need to be stuck down to containers with
waterproof glue or floral Blu-tack. You must
make sure that both the container and the pin
holders are dry before sticking them together.

....

Water mister

To revive and hydrate flowers on jobs.
Very important for things in floral foam
like the giant disco ball.

Raffia

I use it to bind my hand-tied bouquets.

Garden string

I love the brown, rustic type and sometimes
use it to tie posies.

Green waxed wire

Dark green, waxed wire on a roll that I use to
bind bouquets, little posies and buttonholes.
I would be lost without this. It goes everywhere
with me.

Plastic bottles

Always handy to have in case of a non-
watertight container. Cut off the top and slot
inside the container. No-one will ever know.
Empty yogurt pots and ice-cream tubs also
make great DIY liners.

Fine wooden canes

For inserting into stems for extra support
and also handy for spearing fruit and vegetables
that you want to add to arrangements.

Pins

For buttonholes.

Sticky tape

For making grids on the top of vases
and binding the bottom of split stems.

Pretty ribbons

Purely for decoration. I like grosgrain
or velvet ones best.

Brown luggage labels

To add messages to posies.

Plastic vials

These are plastic tubes that you fill with water
to keep a single stem fresh. They have stretchy
caps on the end that you poke the stem through,
keeping it watertight. Very useful for using
in garlands.

Gardening gloves

Invest in a good pair. There's nothing worse
than trying to condition roses and being spiked
by every thorn. Mine never leave my side.

CONTAINERS

As far as I'm concerned, anything with a hole in the top can be used as a container for flowers. One of my biggest joys is hunting for them. Flea markets, charity shops, car boot sales, supermarkets, online . . . You can find them in the oddest places when you're least expecting to find anything. Those ones always seem to be the most treasured finds.

Second-hand shops are container heaven. Look in the kitchen section for cut glass and silver, vintage china tankards and jugs. I'm crazy about lustreware but have never managed to get any especially great deals on this yet. I did, though, find a set of the most delicate crystal tumblers a few months back for less than the price of a coffee. I've used them over and over again. So pleasing!

Building a good collection takes time. It's rare that you'll ever come across a complete set of something but little bits here and there are great. Don't *not* buy something because there's only one of it. I love that mishmash feeling you get from things collected over time. And with flowers, you don't always have to have huge bunches. A single stem picked from the garden or mini posy in a tiny cut glass is so happy-making to wake up to first thing in the morning.

If you find something that you want to use but it's not watertight, all you need to do is slot something inside to hold the water. Plastic water bottles cut down are great for this and come in so many sizes. Alternatively, you can buy bucket liners which are designed especially for this purpose.

If you want to use floral foam in something that isn't waterproof, line it first with cellophane or plastic bags and then sit the foam on top.

....

All of the following can be used in some way
as containers or vessels for displaying flowers.

China mugs

Jugs

Drinking glasses. Look out for
coloured glass in particular.

Candle holders

Shells

Antique spice containers –
I love vintage enamel ones

Glass pickle jars
(your local fish and chip shop would
probably give you theirs when
they've used the contents if you
ask nicely).

Teapots

Empty tin cans – think about
painting or spray-painting them
after removing all the paper.

Jam jars (your local supermarket
will be full of pretty glass jars. Look
in more places than just the
jam aisles. I've found beautiful
cornichon, mustard and coffee jars.
Foreign supermarkets always feel
even more exciting.)

China sugar pots.
Just remove the lid.

Vintage marmalade pots

Vintage mustard pots

Test tubes

Light bulbs

Candlestick holders

Wooden crates

Science beakers

Ceramic bowls

Jelly moulds

Buckets and milk pails

Vintage fire buckets

Egg cups

Baskets

Milk churns

Scooped out vegetables –
artichokes, pumpkins, cabbages

Vintage toilet cistern

Milk bottles

Wooden wine boxes

Birdcages

Colanders

Vintage spirit barrels/kegs

Olive oil tins

Ceramic cachepots

Metal watering cans

Antique children's trucks and
lorries make very cool planters.

Tea tins

Empty glass bath oil bottles

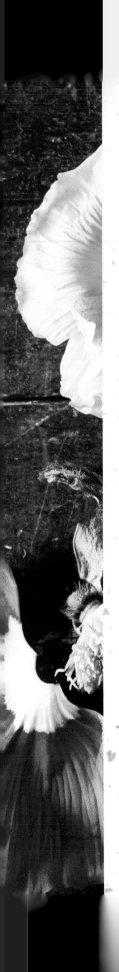

THANK YOU

With three small boys, a new pub and my floral business to run, taking on this book has sometimes felt pretty insane. Saying that, I have loved every single second of it. When I work with clients as much as they listen to my ideas and suggestions, more often than not they are coming to me with a very clear vision of what it is they want me to create. Writing this book has been such a joy because I've been completely free to dream up whatever I've wanted to. I've been allowed to run free, no restraints. Kyle, thank you, this is all down to you. Thank you for trusting me and giving me this incredible opportunity.

Emma Mitchell. Photographer extraordinaire. As cool as a cucumber 24/7. I adore working with you, thank you for getting me, *again!*

Vicky Orchard. My wonderful editor. Thank you for letting me run wild and for being so calm when I've felt anything but.

Kate Corbett-Winder. Mama, thank you for *everything* you do for me; for being my co-writer/editor/stylist/arranger/adviser. I would not have a clue what I was doing without you. Thank you for everything.

Chazzy. For your encouragement and love. You are mega and I love you very, very much.

Wolf, Rafferty and Kit. Thank you for putting up with me staring at a screen for hours on end instead of playing with you. Thank you for the treasures you always bring me. I love them. And **you**, very, **very** much.

Bridget Elworthy. You and your flowers are truly inspiring. Thank you SO much for letting me with work with you both. I'm already excited about your next dahlia crop!

Suze, the most wonderful mother-in-law of all time. I don't know how you manage to look after us all like you do. The way you put your life on hold to help us out 24/7 *and* still smile about it *and* make me chocolate mousse *and* wade through towers of ironing *and* be used as a tackling post by the boys is astonishing. We are SO lucky to have you.

And to Robin, a special thank you for letting us take Suze away from you so much. You are a very patient and generous man.

To Bridget Buchannan, Sophie and James Perkins, Lou, Bea and Honour Nicholls and Charlotte and Harry LJ, thank you very much for letting us invade your beautiful homes to shoot this book. It's a big ask and you were all so generous letting me wander around willy-nilly all day. Thank you.

Katie Shepherd. This book would not exist without you. Thank you for looking after the Cubs day in and day out. You are MEGA. Thank you a million times over, I would be lost without you.

Chloe and Eddie. For arriving on my doorstep with armfuls of home-cooked meals. You are the most wonderful friends.

My lovely neighbours, Caroline and Allan for your gorgeous Japanese anenome donations.

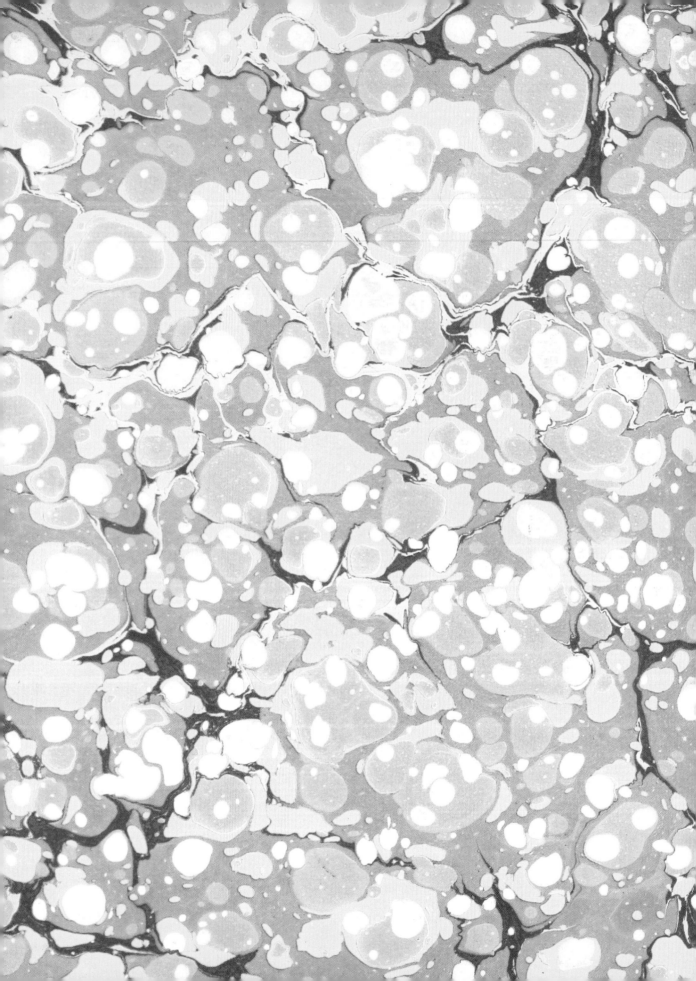